CELESTIAL FIRE

A RECENT AWAKENING IN EASTERN EUROPE

MAUREEN WISE

MUDIAD EFENGYLAIDD CYMRU · EVANGELICAL MOVEMENT OF WALES · SERVING THE CHURCH

In this book Maureen shares with us something of her own personal recollections of this spiritual awakening, yet much of what she records, often verbatim, is the result of her interviewing in 2017 some 40 people, many of them pastors, about their personal experience and recollections of the revival. Read these testimonies and learn what life was like for believers under Communism, the amazing answers to prayer that came through this spiritual awakening, and the way in which the fruit continues today. May your reading lead you to join in Maureen's own prayer and hope for our own land: 'May we be inspired to cry out to the Lord in deep repentance and faith that He might visit these islands in saving power once more!'

— HECTOR MORRISON, HIGHLAND THEOLOGICAL COLLEGE

Here is a humbling, challenging account of what the Lord has done in power in Moldova. In the context of fierce persecution by the Soviet Union and severe restrictions on Christians, we read of the dedication, suffering and love of Moldovan believers. From 1988-2000, a powerful revival swept through Moldovan churches bringing many to Christ. This is a must-read book and a challenge to pray for revival in our churches.

— ERYL DAVIES, ELDER, HEATH EVANGELICAL CHURCH, CARDIFF; RESEARCH SUPERVISOR, UNION SCHOOL OF THEOLOGY

We have here an informed and much-needed synthesis of the events that proceeded, characterized and followed the God-given blessing of revival in the Republic of Moldova, a small country in the eastern part of Europe. Using the stories of many people Maureen's book judiciously describes, in a very simple and effective way, how important it is for us to know that revival comes from God and that we are responsible to promote it for God's glory and the conversion of many. Maureen's book will, I am sure, become a standard introduction to its subject and, therefore, I rejoice and recommend it to all. It will uplift and edify your faith if you read it!

— DR. DINU MOGA, GENERAL MANGER OF FACLIA PUBLISHING HOUSE; DIRECTOR OF EMANUEL SCHOOL OF PRACTICAL THEOLOGY AT EMANUEL UNIVERSITY OF ORADEA, ROMANIA

Maureen Wise has given us a well-researched, gripping account of God's powerful activity in a little known part of Eastern Europe. The book first gives moving testimonies of the lives of Christians under Communism and then of those who were converted during the spiritual awakening and sets out the many benefits that have resulted from this wonderful divine visitation. What is more, the author has herself lived through these revival years and that becomes obvious from the way she writes. Read this book. You will not only be more informed but it will do your soul good and will encourage you to pray for such times of refreshing wherever you live.

— PHILIP H EVESON, PASTOR AND AUTHOR

ISBN: 978-1-78397-243-2

The Evangelical Movement of Wales works in both Welsh and English and seeks to help Christians and churches by:

• running children's camps and family conferences

• providing theological training and events for ministers

• running Christian bookshops and a conference centre

• publishing magazines and books

Bryntirion Press is a ministry of EMW. Past issues of EMW magazines and sermons preached at our conferences are available on our web site: www.emw.org.uk

Published by Bryntirion Press, Waterton Cross Business Park, South Road, Bridgend CF31 3UL, in association with:

EP BOOKS, EP Books (Evangelical Press) Registered Office: 140 Coniscliffe Road, Darlington, Co Durham DL3 7RT

admin@epbooks.org www.epbooks.org

EP BOOKS are distributed in the USA by:

JPL Books, 3883 Linden Ave. S.E., Wyoming, MI 49548

order@jplbooks.com www.jplbooks.com

MUDIAD EFENGYLAIDD CYMRU
YN GWASANAETHU'R EGLWYS
EVANGELICAL MOVEMENT OF WALES
SERVING THE CHURCH

O Thou who camest from above
The pure celestial fire to impart,
Kindle a flame of sacred love
On the mean altar of my heart!

There let it for Thy glory burn
With inextinguishable blaze,
And trembling to its source return
In humble prayer and fervent praise.

Jesus, confirm my heart's desire
To work and speak and think for Thee;
Still let me guard the holy fire,
And still stir up Thy gift in me.

Ready for all Thy perfect will,
My acts of faith and love repeat,
Til death Thine endless mercies seal
And make the sacrifice complete.

— CHARLES WESLEY

CONTENTS

PREFACE

I first went to Moldova in 1998 and found myself in a country where the Lord was working powerfully. People were being converted in every church service I attended and the churches were packed, conversations were full of the Lord and what he was doing in those early years of Gospel freedom. My new-found friends were witnessing everywhere they went, both to acquaintances and to strangers, and people were listening to what they were saying. Preaching services were being held in the open air too, in parks, on street corners. Here were a people who were on fire for God. There was a fervour to their prayers that made a deep impression on me and they were constantly praying! Every possible opportunity of bringing the glory of Christ to men, women and children was being taken. Lives were at full stretch for the Saviour and there was a deep hunger to know about God in the land. Tracts were read eagerly, not thrown away. People were so glad to get hold of a copy of the Scriptures and read the Word with great interest. In the Lord's providence I had been working in an area in Romania in the 1990s which had experienced a powerful, recent revival and I had seen something of the effects of such a movement of the Spirit of God there.

I had known nothing of the work of God in Moldova before I visited there, entering for the first time a little-known country as far as Western Europe is concerned. Moldova is small, economically poor and squeezed between Romania and the Ukraine. In the past it was a 'sister' Republic of the Soviet Union. Its economy collapsed when the Soviet Union fell and a huge migration of Moldovans began as people sought to find work in other places. That migration continues even to this day.

During my years in Moldova I heard many accounts of how the Lord worked there in the 1990s and 2000s and I determined that some of those memories needed to be recorded. Freedom for the Gospel began to arrive towards the end of the 1980s and was more than just an easing of the religious pressures. The new found liberty certainly helped enormously but the 1990s and early 2000s saw a great movement of God's Spirit in the land. This drew untold thousands into the embrace of Christ. Alongside my own personal recollections of the awakening and the countless conversations on the subject I have had with Moldovan friends over the years I have also undertaken a more formal approach to recording the events. During 2017 I interviewed about 40 people, many of them pastors, on their personal recollections of the revival. The interviews typically would last two or three hours and I would type up their accounts word for word with the broadest possible structure of questions as a backcloth. In the process I felt that I was uncovering a spiritual treasure trove and my hope is that I can convey something of that to readers. Much of this book is therefore taken up with verbatim quotes from those interviews.

It had not been my original intention to record very much of the period leading up to the revival, that is pre-1990. My view was that the history of Soviet Christians under the Communist regime had been very thoroughly explored and written up already. I can remember reading countless accounts during the 1970s and 80s particularly, which made me very familiar with their situation. I have had a major re-think about this. It is one thing to read such accounts and it is quite another to be in the same room as a brother or sister in Christ who is recounting what happened in their own family to their own relatives or to themselves. I feel compelled to write up some of those accounts and I hope that you will understand why I have done this. I interviewed pastors and members of both registered and unregistered churches but I have not commented on the separation between these two groups believing that no profitable purpose would be served in doing this. I have a deep respect for brothers and sisters in Christ on both sides of the divide.

The first six chapters of the book use interview material from men and women who lived through the Soviet system and experienced its repression of Christians. This is the period that preceded the revival. Chapters 7 to 12 deal with the awakening itself and its background of economic collapse and mass emigration. The remaining chapters deal with the remarkable fruit of the revival in its numerous forms.

It may well be that the awakening in Moldova is the most recent of its kind in Europe but it has remained largely unknown. I hope these pages will do something to correct that lack of knowledge. I also hope that we will be encouraged to live a life devoted to the Saviour at whatever cost, as did those of whom you will read. May we be inspired to cry out to the Lord in deep repentance and faith that He might visit these islands in saving power once more!

INTRODUCTION

The Gospel arrived in Moldova towards the end of the nineteenth century. By 1888 there were a number of evangelical churches. Baptists formed an identifiable group after 1898 and today they are the largest Protestant denomination in the country. The Baptist Union in Moldova is evangelical.

The first Congress of Evangelical Protestants and Baptists took place in 1927 in Chișinău and drew a few hundred men. The Congress formed a Union with a clear structure and they assumed the name of Evangelical Baptist Christians, drawing together believers of a variety of ethnic origins.

When the revival began in about 1988 it seems that none of the pastors had theological training nor did they have access to theological literature. Not all of them even possessed their own complete copy of the Scriptures at that time. The oppression of the church under the Soviet regime had been harsh and so there was only one open registered church in the capital Chișinău, which has a population of over a million people. The unregistered church in the capital was meeting in the open air, their building having been destroyed by the authorities. Most but not all of the pastors in Moldova would be Arminian in their theology. There is still a great shortage of good theological literature.

The Romanian word for believer means 'repentant one' in English. Repentance of believers and non-believers plays a key part in Moldovan church life. At the end of most services there is a 'call to repentance' when those seeking the Lord after the Word has been preached, will go to the front of the church and kneel and pray out loud in the presence of the congregation. Frequently there will be tears of repentance at this time. During my early years there I can recall that at the end of every service in the large church I attended in the city about 30 or 40 people would go out to the front of the church and kneel and pray in repentance. Importance is attached to 'the repentance of the repentant ones' meaning the continual repentance of believers.

Prayer and fasting is a regular discipline for Moldovan Christians and the Baptist churches set aside each Wednesday for prayer and fasting across the land. They will pray for specific matters, one of which is now that the Lord will visit the land with another great awakening.

Moldovan Christians have much spiritual stamina. Services will often last for two or three hours often with more than one preaching message. In winter many of the village churches do not have heating but this does not act as a deterrent to attendance. Times of congregational prayer often result in prayers tumbling out one after another in quick succession. In the city churches there will be no gaps in the praying and a great eagerness to pray. It is common to see a whole congregation on their knees crying out to the Lord.

Adult baptism is usually preceded by catechism classes, a discussion and questioning by the church council and then a congregational vote giving their assent to an individual's readiness for baptism. It is necessary to have been baptised as an adult to become a church member and to take part in the Lord's Supper. Church discipline is fairly rigorous.

When Christians meet together on any occasion conversations will be full of the Lord in the most natural way possible. Every opportunity will be taken to pray together. At Easter, in common with some other countries, Moldovans will use the Christian form of greeting in place of a general, 'Hello, how are you?' One person will say, 'The Lord is risen!' and the person with whom they are talking will reply, 'He is risen indeed!' This continues for 40 days following Easter Sunday. I can remember, not so long ago at Easter, I was in a village and some children passed me on a bike. They shouted out to me as they passed, 'The Lord is risen!' I joyfully and loudly replied, 'He is risen indeed!' There is a general respect for God in the land, the Orthodox church having a significant following.

Moldovans are musically gifted people and most churches of any size would have a choir and maybe an orchestra of mandolins or balalaikas and other instruments. Membership of a choir is restricted to church members and is considered a form of Christian service that is taken very seriously.

There is an emphasis in the churches on the imminent return of the Christ in His second coming. All the Christians that I know would be looking for His appearing and expectant that He is returning soon. Along with this expectation is a consciousness of needing to be ready to meet with Him, of living lives worthy of Him and daily repentance from every known sin.

I have struggled to find accurate statistics about the exact size of church growth during the revival—the figures that I was given varied considerably and the mass migration that took place during the revival and subsequently obscured much of the real church growth. Whatever the true figures there is evidence to be seen, both in terms of the spectacular proliferation of churches in the capital and throughout the country and in the depth of Christian experience easily observed in many believers

Throughout the book I have prefixed the names of those whom I interviewed with the title 'Brother' or 'Sister.' This is because that would be a normal form of address between Christians in Moldova and it is one I use all the time. To omit those titles feels disrespectful and I hope the reader will understand. Whilst the religious context is different from ours in many ways, my hope is that those differences will not obscure the reader's understanding of what, by any account, was a great work of the Holy Spirit there.

Although Moldova is now in the aftermath of the awakening of which you will read, the spiritual temperature is still much higher there than in the UK. Very many of the people I know were converted in the revival. It shows in their selflessness and sacrifice; in their prayer life and witnessing and in the depth of their fellowship with a Saviour who loved them and washed them from their sins in His own blood. Their life centres on Christ and their conversation is full of Him.

Then they that feared the Lord spake often one to another: and the Lord hearkened, and heard it, and a book of remembrance was written before him for them that feared the Lord, and that thought upon his name. Malachi 3:16

TIMELINE

- 1918 Romania took control of Basarabia
- 1922 Stalin became General Secretary of the Communist Party
- 1927 First Congress of Protestant Evangelicals held in Moldova and the Baptist Evangelical Union formed
- 23rd July 1941 Germany conquered Basarabia
- August 1944 The Soviets occupied Moldova and it became the Soviet Socialist Republic of Moldavia
- 1953 Death of Stalin
- 1960 The Soviet authorities pressured Evangelical Baptist

Leaders to issue a Letter of Instruction to local
congregations restricting many religious freedoms. This led
to a denominational split in August 1961 between
unregistered and registered congregations

- 4th March 1977 The great Vlancea earthquake affects
Moldova
- 10th November 1982 Brezhnev dies and Andropov comes
to power
- February 1985 Death of Andropov. Chernenko assumes
power until late 1985
- 1985 Gorbachev became General Secretary of the
Communist Party in the USSR
- January 1987 A month of prayer and fasting in the
Moldovan churches for religious liberty and freeing of
Christian prisoners
- June 1988 Celebration of 1000 years since the first Russian
baptisms
- 31st August 1989 A language law proclaimed that the
Romanian language written in the Latin script was to be the
language of state
- March 1990 First free elections in Moldova
- May 1990 Moldova becomes an Independent Republic
- 1990 Gorbachev becomes President
- 27th August 1991 Moldova declares independence
- 1991-1992 Moldovan Civil War between Moldovans, (who
were ethnically Romanian) and Slav separatists, (who were
ethnically Russian or Ukrainian) who feared Moldova would
join with Romania to the West. A bloody inter-ethnic
conflict broke out. Russia's 14th Army provided arms and
sometimes troops to the Slav separatists. July 1992 saw a
cease-fire and the autonomous Dniestr Republic was set
up in Moldova to the east of the River Nistru
- 1995 Găgăuzia is granted territorial autonomy within
Moldova

- 1998 Energy crisis throughout the country; wages and pensions were being paid with considerable delays and corruption was rife in the country. This all had an effect on mass emigration
- 2001 The Communists regained power and remained in political power until 2009
- 2009 Moldova joins the European Union's Eastern Partnership. The Republic of Moldova actively pursues European Union membership
- November 2016 Igor Dodon, a pro-Russian candidate, wins the Presidential elections

I

PART ONE: MEN AND WOMEN WHO SUFFERED IN THE SOVIET SYSTEM

DON'T YOU KNOW ME?

*T*he period immediately preceding the awakening in Moldova was a time when the Soviet Union dominated this little country and when 'scientific atheism' was standard teaching in all educational establishments. Of the men and women I interviewed, those who had become Christians during that period of Soviet rule had all experienced persecution. Typically they understated their sufferings but it was clear that those experiences and the way in which God had drawn near to them had marked them for life. So our story begins with some of their accounts of a time when it was most costly to be a follower of Christ, providing the context in which the revival began.

BROTHER ALEXANDRU

I had arranged to meet a pastor, Brother Alexandru, in his office in the Baptist Union in Chișinău. At the time he was Deputy Bishop of the Baptist Union in Moldova. As noted previously, the Baptist Union in Moldova is thoroughly evangelical; it does, however, have a structure that will not be familiar to many Western believers, with a bishop and deputy bishop appointed every three years. I had not met him before and I entered to find an older man of 62 of short stature and humble demeanour greeting me warmly. I had already learnt from my friends that this was a pastor greatly loved by the saints in Moldova who had served the Lord sacrificially and faithfully for years. He immediately launched into his family's story. By the end of his account I felt that I was on holy ground.

I was born in the Ukraine into a family of Christians. My grandfather was the first missionary in an area in the east of the Ukraine. He was sent to the camps in Siberia for ten years during the hardest years. When he was taken my grandmother was expecting my mother, her fourth child. We heard nothing about him for ten years. He received a sentence of death because he was unable to work anymore. We learnt later that he did receive some letters and he had heard that his daughter had been born.

One day he was stripped naked and taken out to be killed with a group of other men. He was praying on the way to the execution site, 'Lord you can save me like you saved Shadrach, Meshach and Abednego and I have a daughter and I want to see her if it's your will but if not I commit myself into your arms.' While he was praying a doctor from the camp came up to him and took him by the arm and quickly pulled him out of the group. He hid him in the laboratory and he escaped execution. He had been treated by this doctor who was Jewish and the doctor had wanted to save him. He was eventually able to get back to work and he served out his ten year term.

REUNION

At the end of the ten years he came home. He knocked on the door late at night. My grandmother opened the door and a stranger entered the house. In those days there were very many poor souls who would go from house to house asking for food and she thought he was one such and received him as a starving stranger who may need help. He looked at all the children and my mother of course was the youngest daughter. He did not know her. He asked my grandmother, 'Are these all your children?' Then he asked, 'Who else lives here?' (He wanted to know if his mother was still alive.) She replied that her mother-in-law also lived with them. He then asked, 'Where is your husband?' and she replied, 'We have not heard about him for ten years.' She had no idea it was him. She asked him why he was interested in her family. He said, 'Don't you know me?' 'It's the first time I have seen you in my life,' she answered. Then he used her name, 'Mariusa' and her eyes were opened and she cried out, 'Children your father has come back! Your father has come back!' They all embraced him. It was 1948. My mother is still alive and she still remembers that she could not sleep all that night. She wanted to run out into the street and tell everyone, 'I have a father, I have a father!'

My mother married at the age of 17 and I am her first-born. I inherited my grandfather's big Bible—it is 120 years old. When he was arrested my grandmother hid his Bible. I can remember when we used to visit them my grandfather would give me the Bible to read as I was the oldest and my knees were trembling as I read it. I can remember my grandmother saying to him, 'Why don't you let the children go out and play? Why do you want to keep them by you?' He told her that they would have time to play but that he was teaching them what would help them through life and prepare them for eternity. I have become what he prayed for me.

CONVERSION

I was 12 when I repented. The church used to meet in a house which was seven kilometres away from our home and we walked over the hills to get there. The pastor used his house for our meetings and he too had been in prison for ten years. It was in his house that I was converted. My preaching started because of my grandfather. I started to preach at the age of 12. There were hardly any older men in the church at the time and my grandmother said to me, 'Read to us and tell us whatever the Lord has put on your heart.' I read a whole chapter of Matthew and then I proposed that we all kneel and pray. I did not understand what was happening at the time but the Lord met with us and convicted us of our sin and we all cried out to Him. But after that my grandmother told me that the Lord was calling me to be a pastor. And so it was.

My life under the Soviet Union was very difficult. For fifteen years I had to wear a placard round my neck at school as I refused to be a Pioneer [a member of the young Communists]. It was very difficult to study. When I started working I used my first salary to buy a radio to listen to Christian broadcasts from abroad. That was my theological school. It was impossible to go to theological college.

A MEETING WITH MR GREAT HEART

In 1961, following pressure from the Soviet authorities, there was a division between Baptists in the Soviet Union into registered and unregistered churches. The registered churches agreed to some restrictions on church practices whilst the unregistered churches refused to cede to such interference from State authorities. I spoke to men and women from both groups of churches to write this book and hold those on both sides of the divide in very high esteem. In earlier years, the unregistered churches were very successful in spreading news to the West about what was happening to their churches and church leaders under the Soviets. Those effective communication networks led to a great wave of prayer for those brothers and sisters, together with political pressure to ease their situation. My more recent contacts have been mostly, although not exclusively, with brothers and sisters from registered churches and I have realised that they were far from exempt from suffering for the Gospel also.

BROTHER NICOLAE

Brother Nicolae was also in his early 60's and was a pastor in an unregistered church. He, like Brother Alexandru, had known what it was to suffer for Christ and for the Gospel. I spent hours speaking with him while he gently told his story. There was not the slightest trace of bitterness in his attitude as he recounted what had happened to him. He would not elaborate on some of the things that had happened to him and I felt with him, as with some others, that he had known a secret fellowship with the Saviour's sufferings that would remain hidden. This beloved pastor became a 'Mr Great Heart' in my mind. It was clear that he loved his flock and that he loved serving his Saviour. He lives in a village and has a very large extended family and many grandchildren. This was his experience:

> I was called up to the Soviet Army in 1973. (It is amazing how many of my now friends were soldiers in the Soviet Army—our erstwhile enemies!) They told me not to tell anyone about Christ and I refused. I was training to be a member of the Special Forces having always been keen on sports in my youth but they did not allow me to finish the training. I was condemned by a Military Tribunal to three years in prison and I was taken to a camp in Kazakhstan which was 5000 kilometres from my home. When I was sent there I was 20 years old and unmarried. I had so many experiences with God there!
>
> Once I was struck in the back and I still have problems with my back as a result of that blow. Not all of them beat me because they knew that I had been trained in the Special Forces so some of

them were a bit wary of my strength. It was a kind of protection for me.

I was able sometimes to read books in the library there and I read the great Russian authors such as Tolstoy and Dosteyevsky and they occasionally quoted from the Bible in their writings. I wrote down all these quotes from the Bible and used them.

I can remember that some German believers once came to sing Christian songs outside the prison. I was punished as a result of their visit as they thought it was something to do with me and they would not believe that it had not been at my instigation. Although it caused me problems it was a great witness.

I have since received letters from some of my fellow prisoners from those days. One wrote to tell me that he had been converted and was a deacon in his local church and another wrote to tell me that he had also become a Christian. Only the Lord knows what fruit remains from those days.

GREAT WELCOME

I completed my sentence and came back to my church where I received a great welcome. Following my return I was asked to help in translation work. I translated the Bible and our song book from the Latin script into the Cyrillic script and I translated another twenty books including one of Spurgeon's. While I was involved in that work I lived as a fugitive. I disappeared from public view and hid in a place in the forests. The KGB were looking everywhere for me but I hid myself to carry on with the translation work. I had a typewriter there in the woods. Friends would bring me provisions and I would make my own food. It was only very rarely that I could return home. The KGB were always tightening their control on me. They thought I was a spy for the West; they didn't know about the translation work. I decided not to marry until the translation work on the Bible was completed. I was always disappearing then appearing again. There were even rumours that I had left the faith because of this. Only very few people knew what I was doing including a small number of pastors. Even my own father who was also a pastor did not know about the things I was involved in. In the end someone betrayed me but it was too late as the work on the Bible had been finished.

A number of you may have read the book, *Vanya* which was published in 1975. It tells the story of Vanya Moiseyev who was martyred in 1972 whilst serving in the Soviet Army. Pastor Nicolae, about whom you have just read, was converted through Vanya's witness shortly before Vanya's death. Vanya came to speak to the young people in the church which Nicolae attended and they spoke together after the meeting. Nicolae was deeply affected by what he heard and was baptised the same year. So he, like Vanya, had entered the Soviet Army as a baptised believer which marked him out for serious difficulty.

VANYA THE MARTYR AND VLADIMIR HIS BROTHER

I knew that Vanya had lived in Moldova and remembered reading the account of his life and death many years ago. It had made a big impression on me and on the many others who had read it. On making enquiries I discovered that his brother, Vladimir, was still alive and to my enormous sense of privilege and indeed wonder I was able to interview him. I had never imagined that I would meet the brother of someone who was martyred and whose story I had read many years ago. Again Brother Vladimir was in his 60s but in frail health. He was thin and stooped in stature and looked much older than his years. He explained that he was living with his daughter and had been seriously ill of late. I met him first one warm evening, at the end of a packed service in one of the unregistered churches in Chișinău. He welcomed me to their church

9

most kindly and to my astonishment agreed to talk with me during the following week about his brother and about his own experiences. This is what he related to me:

> I am two years older than Vanya and we spent our childhood together. My parents were converted in the church in Slobozia at Christmas when I was 12 years old. I remember that they went to the front crying. My mother was crying out to God for forgiveness. After that we started to go to church every Sunday. It was 12 kilometres on foot but we were never late for a service.

SPIRITUAL BATTLE

> I was called up to the army and I received letters from Vanya when I was in the army. He was baptised before joining the army and he was a member of the church in Tiraspol. While I was doing national service I was called in to see the Commandant who told me that my brother was not willing to take the army oath. I said I could not force him, he was of an age to decide for himself. I was a believer then but not baptised. I was called in a few times to put pressure on him but I would not agree to do so. I returned home eventually and was baptised in 1971. It was soon after that when I received the last letter from Vanya. He wrote to me of a dreadful spiritual battle in which he found himself and asked me not to tell our parents straight away. There was no letter after that. Then two or three days later he was killed. Many army officers came to see him from different units in order to force him to take the oath. He refused and they decided to condemn him to death. It was 1972 and Vanya was serving in the Crimea in Kerch. They said he had drowned in the Azov Sea. I went to where the incident was said to have happened and people told me not to believe what we had been told. They told me that on 16th June a number of KGB men arrived dressed in civilian clothes.

They drowned Vanya but before drowning him he had been terribly tortured.

We asked them to send his body home. They put the body in a sealed, metal coffin but we opened the coffin and took his body out to prepare it for burial. I personally saw his body. There was a Commissar whose job had been to prevent us from opening the coffin. He left when he realised that we were not going to cede to his wishes.

We were all horrified when we saw Vanya's body! He had so many wounds on his body and his face was cruelly beaten. All those who saw his body wrote an open letter which they signed as direct witnesses of what they had seen. Photos were taken also and distributed to many. [I remember seeing one such photo during the 1970's in prayer information received, I believe from Friedenstimme]. My parents and all our relatives were crying all the way to the cemetery.

After the funeral I gathered a number of significant documents about Vanya's death and packed them up carefully and took them to Moscow and to Brezhnev at the Kremlin. A brother from Moscow came with me. We had a sense of the Lord being with us. I waited there a long time and a man finally asked me what I wanted and went away again. After a very long time he returned and told me that I should go and that the medical legal team would investigate the death in about three or four weeks. The medical legal team eventually concluded that Vanya had died because of violence. A man named Scorta from the Academy of Science became involved in our case soon afterwards.

Immediately after I arrived back home my mother and I were taken to the Commissar of the police at four in the morning. They let my mother return home but they took my clothes and shoes away and I was imprisoned in an underground cell with one other lad. I was given one glass of water a day and a piece of dry, black bread every other day. The first week I was called in for questioning and they gave me a letter to sign denying all the documents I had left at the Kremlin. I refused because I knew they contained the truth. The second week Scorta came back again for my signature. He told me that if necessary he could just dispose of me so that no-one would ever know what had happened to me. I said that if it was God's will I was ready. He got up and struck me in the face until my nose was broken and the blood was flowing. All this had been directed from Moscow.

By the third week I was starving and he came again to ask for my signature. I refused and he hit me very badly again and they took me back underground to my cell. The man, Scorta, who had beaten me up and interrogated me was killed in a car accident shortly afterwards.

In the fourth week they came to tell me that Scorta had died and that I was going home. They brought my shoes and clothes back and I was amazed to be going home. Years went by. I saw all these things with my own eyes. Communist ideological pressure pursued me until 1990. At work they left me without sufficient shifts to make a living. It was all very, very hard. My parents always struggled financially. My mother died seven years ago at the age of 84. She had lost her sight. But Vanya's death had a profound effect on our fellowship and the after-effects are still being felt. Many repented and were saved because of his testimony.

I was very close indeed to my brother spiritually. I can remember that when we had free time there was a place in the garden where we used to pray together. All our time is under the control of God. He gives us difficult times with persecution and times when we have very little and now He has given us a different time. The Lord said, 'If they hate Me they will hate My disciples also.' The early church knew the truth of that.

Brother Vladimir told me that from time to time he was asked to take groups of young people to visit Vanya's grave and to tell them his story. On one recent occasion a group of young people were visiting from the Ukraine and some of them were converted as a consequence of what they heard.

Two weeks after I spoke with Vladimir Moiseyev in September 2017 he died.

Those interviews with three men who had indeed gone through great tribulation opened a door for me again on the experience of so many Soviet Christians. It reminded me powerfully of things that I had heard of them in earlier years, but on this occasion I was meeting them face to face. Those encounters were in every sense remarkable for me.

The following chapter tells the story of one of the great spiritual giants of the unregistered churches whose Christian life was spent mostly in a time of severe persecution.

2

SOMEONE I NEVER EXPECTED TO MEET!

*A*nother person whom I never expected to meet, let alone interview, was the widow of Mihail Khorev who had been one of the three main leaders of the unregistered church in the Soviet Union alongside Georgi Vins and Gennadi Kruchkov. I could remember Brother Khorev's face from the prayer information received regularly about the unregistered churches. In fact the faces of these three dear brothers remain in my memory from those days. Brother Georgi Vins actually preached in my home church soon after being sent into exile in the West. Each of these three men suffered greatly for the Gospel.

SISTER VERA

This was the story Sister Vera, the widow of Mihail Khorev, recounted:

> God so blessed me because I grew up in a Christian family and my parents were wonderful people. They had a great love for the Lord and His Word. May the Lord so revive us in our day that we would be like them! The hour of prayer at church was always

sacred. On Thursdays and Saturdays my father would leave his work and rush off to worship. Every evening he would read to us from the Bible and tell us about the Lord. We used to learn Bible verses by heart. Through my parents I learnt that the Bible was a holy book. There was such a fear of God in our family and when we prayed or listened to the Word we knew that we were in the presence of the Most Holy One. Life was difficult but we saw that our parents' faith was supernatural and real. We did not want to grieve the Lord either by our words or our actions even as children…

I was born in Truşeni and my home church was there. [Truşeni is the village in which Casa Bucuriei, the first of the Casa Mea houses is situated. It is just outside the capital, Chişinău]. There was great pressure on the church in those days. Many Christian brothers were being sent into exile and prayer houses were being shut. Grigore Rudenca was a great servant of God from our church and in 1948 he was given a ten year sentence. His wife was sent to Siberia and his children were sent to State Orphanages. He came back in 1957 and the members of our church were overjoyed to see him. But the leading minister was not happy as there was a rule that those who had been in prison for political crimes could not be a member of a church until they admitted that they were an enemy of the State. They could not take communion and nobody had the right to communicate with them. But when Brother Grigore saw the love of the members he was very happy and the church did give him the right to preach and sing in the choir.

In 1960 two letters came from Moscow. There was an instructive letter and a more secret letter for pastors. The content was very detailed. You were not allowed to preach about eternal suffering and hell and there were edicts about prayer; children and young people were forbidden to attend services etc. The church council met and said the letter should be signed but Grigore Rudenca said he could not sign it as it was against the Word of God. Someone came from Moscow and a members' meeting was organised and he was excluded from the church. Two of the brothers raised questions about why he had been excluded. Two days later all three were arrested at work and sentenced to fifteen days imprisonment. They were accused falsely of causing a great upset in the church and of trying to beat up the pastor. It was all lies.

Many of the leading brothers were excluded from churches at that time. In 1960, 300 churches were closed. There was a group who had been excluded who started to meet in houses and they included children and young people in their meetings. That happened all over the place and it was how the unregistered churches started...

My mother was keen for each of us to have some kind of profession – she didn't want us to work on a collective farm. She sent me to medical school in Bender. I thought I would not pass the entrance exam but I did and I was accepted.

During collectivization they had confiscated all our goods including our cart and stores. We did not have enough money and I needed to work to get through medical training. I was employed twice a week at night in Accident and Emergency at the hospital.

PRESSURE AT MEDICAL SCHOOL

It was not too important then to be a Komsomolist [The Komsomol was a Communist Party Young People's organisation, for the age range 14 to 28]. It became more important later. During the fourth year of medical studies they started to put pressure on me to join the Komsomol. This was in 1953. I was called in a few times. Having read the statutes of the Komsomol I learnt that I would have to be involved in ideological education and I knew that I could not do that. At that time there was a pastor responsible in our church who was very tied up with the State KGB. I went to him to seek his advice and he told me to join the Komsomol and get on with my education. I knew I could not agree.

There was going to be a big meeting and I was expected to explain to everyone present why I did not want to join. I had been studying for four years and it was hard to come to terms with the fact that I might well leave with nothing to show for it. But I knew that I could not leave the Lord. My father came to visit me and I shared with him that I found myself in a great battle. He opened the Bible and read 'if we deny Him, He will also deny us'. He warned me to remain strong and he quietened me. He knelt down and prayed for me and told me I would find work.

There were 300 students at the meeting that was arranged and all the lecturers as well! An official came from the Party to explain how important membership was and that there was a student who was not prepared to join the Komsomol. I stood up in the full auditorium to say why I would not join. I remembered that my father was praying for me with his Bible in front of him.

I said that I had read the Statutes of the Komsomol and that they said that you were to enter the organisation of your own free will. I said that I did not want to enter. A student got up and said he had known me for seven years and that I had never missed a lecture and studied hard and he questioned why I should be held to account because I was not in the Komsomol. Another girl got up who belonged to the Komsomol and she said she knew me and she did not understand why someone had to be forced to enter the Komsomol. The Party official said he would return but he did not and the matter ended there. It was wonderful to see how the Lord worked. I told my father about it all and he told me never to be afraid of the face of men...

A WEDDING INVITATION!

As a young woman Vera happened to be in Leningrad (now St Petersburg) for two days. Mihail Khorev led a service which she attended. He invited her to visit the Hermitage (a very large museum) with him. On the way there he said to her that he wanted to invite her to his wedding. She asked him who he was going to marry and he replied, 'You are the bride!' He told her he realised it was all new to her but he asked her to pray about it and let him know her decision. They went to the Hermitage but Vera said she remembered nothing of the museum because her mind was so preoccupied! She told her parents of his offer and they said, 'If he fears and serves the Lord, may the Lord bless you.' Vera did not reply for two months.

The KGB came to see me at work because I was friends with Brother Khrapov who had just been arrested again. They told me I had a link with an enemy of the State. They came to see where I lived—it was a simple room with a Bible and an album with photos. Khorev said I would be tried with Khrapov—they were good friends. I sent a telegram to Mihail Khorev and agreed to marry him. Two days later the Prosecutor called me in about the telegram contents...

We married in Truşeni. The pastor told us we could only have the number of visitors who would fit into the house. I would not accept this and in the end many came to our wedding. The ceremony took place inside the house on 13th June 1961 and then we had a meal outside. My father was a deacon in that church for 30 years and a week after the wedding my parents were excluded from the church.

A year earlier in 1960 they had told us that we could be baptised at night. We had to reply to twenty questions using the Word of God as our responses. At midnight there was questioning before the baptism and at 1 a.m. we set off on foot and at 3 a.m. we were baptised...

PERSECUTION, PRISON SENTENCES AND PUNISHMENTS

Persecution was starting up again in many places in the 60s. Prison sentences were often three years. They took away children from parents and placed them in orphanages. I remember one mother had been converted and she was very active in telling everyone about the Lord. They told her not to speak but she did not stop and they arrested her and gave her a four year sentence and sent her five children to a State Orphanage. Her husband was left behind. He was a believer but not as active as his wife. All five children became Christians. Some families suffered very much.

They arrested my husband in 1966 in Moscow and accused him of being out of work. [If you were without work for over a month you could be arrested]. My husband was serving the unregistered churches and travelled a great deal...

It was decided that a delegation of Christians should be sent to Moscow including five of the leaders to ask for a meeting with Brezhnev to present all the evidence of suffering and injustice for Christians. They stayed there in Moscow for a day and sang and prayed. The next day they were told that Brezhnev had left. Many buses arrived. About 500 people were praying on their knees and singing and they took them all from Red Square to prisons, pulling their hair and treating them roughly. The next day my husband and Brother Vins went to see who was in prison. They were both arrested also. Many were arrested but others always took their places.

In 1966, 270 were arrested and the Council of Prisoners' Relatives was formed. Their task was to find out the situation of the prisoner's families—their health and finances and family difficulties and to take care of them. The first woman to lead the group was arrested and her children were taken into State care and then Lidia Vins became the leader. They asked me to join them but I refused and they reminded me that my husband was in prison and asked me if others should be taking care of him if I was not. They reminded me that I was free from work on Saturday and Sunday. So I joined them. We found out a lot of information about the families of our prisoners and we submitted a lot of material to the Government. This included Scriptural material and we used the opportunity to tell them of the Gospel and remind them that a day was coming when they would have to give account to God. I was a member of that Council for fifteen years. We had strong links particularly with believers in Germany and there were demonstrations on our behalf abroad. Eventually Lidia Vins was also imprisoned...

Many sisters who were involved in Sunday school work were arrested. My husband was released in 1969 and came home. He was called back for questioning after six months but he remained home for a year.

My husband was either in prison or on the run and rarely seen. He was blind in one eye and would have had invalid status. He was always in the Lord's work. The Soviet Union was a very big country and he was in different places all the time. He used to come home and they would come looking for him. There would be hundreds looking out for him on the stairs to our flat and two cars with their lights switched on outside the flats, determined to catch him. Once he went to his sister's in Leningrad and they arrested him there at 1 a.m. in the morning and took him to prison again in January 1980.

Our church met in the open air in all weathers for five years in Chişinău and they took the tent we used three times. We stood in the cold and rain and snow... They destroyed our house and took all the belongings and put them in a car. They gave us one room in a family hostel. It had one window facing north. They took everything. We prayed. We knew that the Lord knew everything…

SEARCHING IN SIBERIA

My husband received another prison term in Siberia and I went to see him there with Sister Clava… I was told that he had been sent to Yakutia. An order had come from Moscow to send him there—as far away as possible. I wanted to give him some warm clothing and wondered how I could do this. We discovered that his train would go through Sverdolovsk. I went there with Sister Clava with clothes for him. We went to the prison and found out that he was being transported then and could not receive anything. We knew that the train would go through Novosibirsk and we went there and waited at the station. There were so many trains coming and going. We waited there a whole day and night but his train did not arrive. Then we went to see the pastor in Novosibirsk because we did not know what to do. He went to see a sister from his church who worked in the railway station. She was hesitant to help as she was afraid of losing her job but she did find out that the train was due at 6 a.m. next morning. It was the post train. We were so glad and then we rested a bit and we went the next morning to meet the train. The carriage had tiny slits and so many were peering out of the slits. I called out his name again and again and they asked me why I was shouting. They told me he was still in Omsk.

We went back to the prison in Omsk and discovered that he was there. We asked for a meeting with the Chief Prison Officer. We were so tired. I was crying but I could not help it. They agreed for us to see the boss and I explained it all and he was amazed. 'He arrived last night and his wife arrives this morning? How did you know?' We explained that we were believers and we told him that we had come with clothes for him. I was told that he would remain there for his whole sentence. They let me leave the clothing but they would not allow me to see him then. There was a big gathering of believers in Omsk and we met up with them. My husband was in prison there for five years. I was allowed to see him after a month had gone by...

They told my husband he would never get out of prison and if he did he would be left without friends. He was imprisoned often in the worst part of the prison in the punishment cell. It was very narrow indeed—only 25 centimetres wide with bars on the floor so that you could neither lie down nor stand. The only place he could kneel was near the door. He would be allowed out of there only for a day or two and then he would be returned to the punishment cell. He was there for so long. And the temperature was only 8°C at its warmest. He forgot the names of his children and he even lost consciousness there sometimes. It was so dark in that cell.

THE LORD DEFENDED THEM

My meeting with Sister Vera Khorev lasted many hours and took place in her house in a village near Chișinău on a warm, early autumn day. The house was surrounded by a well-tended garden which despite advanced years she enjoyed looking after. She was living on her own and found the days sometimes a little lonely despite having many friends, but she was shortly going to visit one of her sons in America. Sister Khorev explained to me that her husband had lived only for a short time in this beautiful, tranquil setting before his death. His photo was in a prominent place at the entrance to the first room. She recounted the events in an animated, gripping way and was constantly speaking of the way that the Lord had defended them and strengthened them in every time of trial. Her account of her journey through Siberia to help her husband gives some indication of her tenacity and of her love for her husband. The distances covered were immense by any standards as were the hardships endured. She shared her husband's fearless stand for the Gospel. Her long-term involvement with the Council of Prisoners' Relatives was an indication of her boldness and courage. All these qualities shone through still whilst I was speaking with her.

There follows a story of Christian work amongst women in Moldova during the twentieth century and the suffering of an early pioneer, together with the recollections of three pastors about their families' experiences during the same century. My hope is that this will give us a deeper understanding of this pre-revival era and the way that God was working then.

3

A WIDOW'S RECOLLECTIONS

SISTER OLGA

*S*ister Olga was in her 75th year when I interviewed her and she was a widow. We met on the veranda of her city house surrounded by flowers and summer warmth. She was converted at the age of 14 and baptised at 3.00 a.m. on 6th July 1956 as at that time the Communists had a law which said that one had to be 30 years old before you could be baptised. Although unpretentious, there was a nobility about her character and a richness in her Christian experience and service which awed me.

•

In that same summer of 1956 we young people were so blessed by meeting a sister who had recently returned from Siberia where she had spent fifteen years in prison for the Word of God. She had been arrested in 1941 together with the pastor of the church and the deacons. The pastor was killed and the deacons all went to Siberia and were killed too. They took Sister Lidia to be interrogated and she saw two soldiers holding a man underneath his arms dragging him along. It was the pastor. He was so badly beaten she did not recognise him but she recognised his voice. He said to her, 'My journey is finished but you will return.' What he said was prophetic—he did die but Sister Lidia returned to serve again after many years.

PRISON

For ten years of her prison sentence she had no right to correspond so nobody knew if she was dead or alive. After serving the ten years of her sentence they added another five years. She was in prison with many hardened criminals and their work was felling trees in the forests. One woman there had grown up in an orphanage and got involved in theft. After her trial she swore that she would kill the judge who had convicted her and when she was released she killed him. She told Sister Lidia that she could not sleep because of this. She kept thinking about what she had done. One night she nearly strangled Sister Lidia. Lidia told her of Christ and the two thieves who were crucified with Him and the woman asked her, 'That means He can forgive me?' Sister Lidia said that He could and the woman was converted.

Sister Olga went on to say that, 'I can still remember that Sister Lidia was full of the power of the Holy Spirit and she exhorted us to be faithful, to read the Word of God every day and to pray and to be ready to tell anyone of the hope that it is in us. That meeting was such a means of strengthening us all as young people despite the fact that many of us did not have a Bible of our own then. I later discovered that her name was Lidia Căldăraru.'

A brother said about Sister Lidia, 'I can remember when Sister Lidia came to speak she encouraged the whole church. What an influence! We thought that when she came out of prison we would need to care for her but she came out full of zeal to serve the Lord.'

A WORK AMONGST WOMEN

The first Baptist Congress in Besarabia [a former name for Moldova], took place in 1927. Sister Lidia was 21 then and she was chosen to lead the work with women and children in the Basarabian churches. By 1978 she was 72 years old and unwell. One Sunday in March 1978 she invited all the sisters in the church to a meeting and she told us that the Lord had revealed to her that she was going to glory that year and that I was to take over the work. I told her that I was completely inadequate to the task and didn't have any of the necessary gifts. I was even thrown out of school because I refused to join the Komsomolists. She told me that the Lord would teach me. She died on September 23rd that year. She was very special—the Lord revealed to her what He was about to do.

I learnt at her feet—she had so many messages used of God for the sisters.

On one occasion she told me that I was going to bring the message to the sisters on the coming Thursday. I was expecting my fourth child. There was no way you could refuse her. I cried out to the Lord for help and I prayed for a Word from Him.

The Communist authorities in those days were always asking what was happening in church. They would question my husband and slam their fists on the table and threaten him that he would disappear and nobody would know what had happened to him. There were countless interrogations in those days and the pastors were always being interrogated. There were always secret police in the services. My husband feared God. Two of my husband's brothers were sentenced to ten years in prison. One served six years and the other three years. When Stalin died they were released.

After freedom for the Gospel came, many women from the

world repented. The first conference for women in our country took place in November 1990. In May 1992 I was set aside officially for the women's work in Moldova. I have seen the miracles of God at every step.

It was deeply moving to hear the account of Sister Lidia's life. Her name would be unknown to most people these days but each step of her journey was known to God. There is now a thriving women's work in Moldova and Sister Olga who spoke with me is still very actively engaged in serving the Lord.

I spoke with others of those earlier times. It was interesting that a number recounted memories of their fathers having been pastors and of what they had observed as children.

A FAMINE FOR THE WORD OF GOD

A pastor named Brother Serghei who is in his 60s spoke of his vivid memories of the persecution but also of the deep fellowship between believers that existed. He had watched the struggles of his father who had been a pastor. We met in his church in Chişinău and he stood to pray before our discussion and when it was completed, asking God to use what was spoken to glorify Christ.

Prior to the 1990s there was a severe lack of Bibles for individual Christians. It was most unusual for Christians to have a Bible then. I am one of a third generation of pastors in our family. My grandfather was a pastor in the village of Udobnoe in the region of Odessa during the time of Stalin. My father was a pastor from 1966 to 1985. I never dreamt I would be called to be a pastor—I had learnt how hard it was. I can remember times when my father left home and we did not know if he would return. Sometimes he would be gone all night. Often the pastor and the church council did not share things with the congregation as it was too dangerous.

In about 1970 my father received news that he would meet some American Mennonites. They had to meet at night as the KGB followed Western visitors in those days. The Mennonites gave us some very small New Testaments which were printed on very thin paper. Nobody knew where they had come from but they brought such blessing to many families. There were no theological books at all. There would be one Gospel available to a few pastors from which to prepare messages and they had to hand it on to the next preacher once they had used it.

Teachers and school heads used to come to church to see which children were in church. The parents were told that it was not permitted for children to attend the church. We were subsequently made examples of at school and humiliated. In the class that I was part of as a child in school, out of 26 pupils, 12 were from Christian families.

But during those times our churches were 'boiling hot' ['on fire' but I have translated the word he used literally]. Believers needed very close fellowship with the Lord because from Him alone came our strength and He was our only hope. We had only the Lord to help us – we had nothing else. And we had such a desire for fellowship with God. How we needed it! And the Christians showed great zeal for the Lord. That was a time when we knew the Lord looking after us.

TWO BROTHERS WHO BECAME PASTORS

I interviewed two brothers, both of whom had become pastors. They are both in their late 40s and now hold great responsibilities —one for a large church and the other as a leader in the Bible College. Both are powerful characters and I listened intently as I heard the story of their respective lives and ministries. The experiences of their father had left an indelible impression on them both. This was the testimony of the brother who is pastor of a large church:

> I was born into a family of Baptists with eleven children. My father was a pastor from 1962 to 1993. He was persecuted and the family suffered a lot. Not one of the children wanted to go into the ministry because we had seen so much. They used to arrest our father during the night and we didn't know when he would come back. People were scared. He did not want to cause panic in the church so he did not tell people what was happening to him but he used to tell only a very small group of brothers. It was very difficult for us materially. I would use some shoes in the morning and then my sister would use the same shoes in the afternoon to go to school. It was the same with our boots.

His brother, Mihai, elaborated on their father's experiences:

> My father spent five years from 1943 to 1948 in the Russian camps during the time of Stalin. He became a pastor in Antoneşti in 1958. My father was such an example for me! The Communist authorities confiscated the church building and my father wrote letters to Moscow protesting against the confiscation. Some of his letters have been found in the Baptist Union archive recently. The Communists offered to return the keys of the church three times but on each occasion they changed their minds. On the third of these occasions my father was asked to go the next day to collect the keys which he did, only to discover that the church building had been bulldozed and nothing remained. That was in 1962. From a young age I understood clearly that there was an inherent hypocrisy in the Communist system—they said one thing but acted altogether differently. I had twenty years to study how this worked.

The sheer resilience of those I spoke to struck me, together with their perseverance in Christian service in such a harsh context. Despite great hardships they had all pressed on to know the Lord and were still faithful and fruitful in His work. Sister Olga, who was the oldest, concluded her story with the following words:

> Old age is beautiful and it is a time of autumn reaping. We are reaping all the harvest now. Don't think about your illnesses—serve the Lord. When we have much to suffer the Lord is with us. He gives strength. He leads us all the way.

In the next chapter, five older Christians recall their childhood memories.

4

MEMORIES FROM CHILDHOOD AND BEYOND

I was fascinated to listen to five other older Christians who were members of the unregistered church as they recounted their childhood memories. They all grew up at a time when children were not legally allowed to go to church. They were picked out for humiliation and punishment at school. Very often they would automatically receive poor marks and higher education was usually closed to them because they did not belong to Communist youth organisations. Churches were being destroyed and Christians would gather in homes clandestinely.

SISTER ALA

Sister Ala was in her 60s and spoke graphically of those times. I met her on a warm summer's afternoon in her home. Lots of black and white photos were displayed round the room from the times she was describing. She related her story:

> I was about 3 years old and children were not allowed to be in the church then. It was 1960 and we children used to go into the church through the back door. Many children stayed at home.

Amongst the children of those times many became pastors. At school they used to call me names all the time. Everyone knew that I was a Christian. We started meeting in homes. Not many knew where we were meeting and it was only on the way to the meeting that someone would whisper which house we were going to use.

During the 1970s we used to meet in a tent. The church had about 200 members by the 80s and then in 1986 a bulldozer was sent to destroy the church building. The police often broke into our services and made us all go home. But from a spiritual point of view the church was strong then. We prayed much and although we suffered harsh persecution our faith was very strong. Brother Khorev was one of the pastors but he was rarely able to come to the meetings as he was often in prison or in hiding. So many brothers were arrested in those days including those involved in literature such as Brother Oleg, Brother Pruteanu, Brother Vasea, Brother Tașcă, Brother Mihail and Brother Ion Zaharovici. My sister-in-law was arrested and sisters involved in secret printing press work were sent to the Rusca prison. Many brothers and sisters went to prison a few times. We prayed as though we were in bonds with those who were in prison. We had a very strong fellowship in prayer in those days.

WE GOT OVER THE FENCE AND WENT IN!: BROTHER GRIGORE

A beloved pastor in his 60s, Brother Grigore, also related events from his childhood:

I was born into a Christian family in Chișinău. My father was a pastor. We used to go to the church near the station. In 1961 the letter came with the new instructions that children were not able to attend church. I was 6 and my brother was 7. They told us we could not go into the church but we got over the fence and went in! I attended that church until 1966 when I left because the brothers would not let the young people attend and would perform baptisms only with the agreement of the State authorities. We were not allowed to preach at weddings or funerals.

We used to meet in houses. There were about seven or eight houses in the city we used to use including our house in Poşta Veche. The police often used to come to our services and told us we were breaking the law and fined the householder. They were always searching the premises for Christian literature. In 1972 or 73 we decided to meet in a tent at Poşta Veche. After three months they would destroy the tent and for five years we met in the open air. Sometimes in the summer we would meet in the woods near Durleşti and we would hold communion services there and sometimes weddings. Our own wedding service took place in a tent.

I was the director of the church choir for 30 years. I had graduated from music school and when I did my exam I got top marks and as a result I should have been able to enter the Conservatory. However someone on the Entry Commission asked for my documents and crossed out my application and told me my education was finished. He was from the KGB. But I thank the Lord that I had a choir of 60 in the church. That became for me the best conservatory of all.

A WHITE HANDKERCHIEF: SISTER NATALIA

Speaking to a fellow lecturer, dear Sister Natalia, in the Bible College where I also taught for a number of years, I discovered a part of her past of which I had no idea previously. Her parents had emigrated to the United States some years earlier and her father, to whom she had been very attached, had died there. I had heard from so many of the high regard in which her father, who was a pastor, was held. Others had recounted to me the risks he had taken for the Gospel and of his passion to lead others to Christ. This was his daughter Natalia's account:

I was born in 1971. Both my parents were believers as were their parents also. My parents attended an unregistered church and when I was one year old my father was ordained as a pastor. During my childhood our church was destroyed five times. I remember the bulldozers coming. I was 10 years old when my father went to prison for the first time. I can remember three policemen and six dogs coming for him. These are the kind of memories I grew up with—I remember those things very well. Just two hours before his trial my mother was informed of what was happening and she was called as a witness. If we waved a white handkerchief from our balcony it was a sign for the believers to pray and we did that then. They would not let us into the court room. My father received a term of two and a half years but he was released after six months in 1984.

AN EARTHQUAKE AND AN AWAKENING: SISTER VALEA

This is Sister Valea's story. She was a widow in her 60s whose family I knew well. We chatted in her home in the countryside on a seriously cold day! But again, until I interviewed her I had hardly any idea of the things that she had previously experienced. As she recounted her story I was astounded to hear some of the events that she had lived through:

I am from Besarabia. My mother was a Baptist believer and my father was Orthodox. I was born in 1953. By the time I was in Class 9 I knew that I wanted to learn a profession. I had a fear of God but the secret of the Gospel had not been revealed to me yet. From 1970 to 1973 I studied in medical school and this necessitated my belonging to the Komsomolists. My mother was very sad about this.

After graduating I came back to my village to work and a year later on 4th March 1977 there was a very big earthquake. I was terrified—the earth was moving like the waves of the sea. I knelt and prayed until morning. I understood that there was a God and I came to Him in repentance that night. I was so thankful that I had not died unsaved.

My father-in-law was an Orthodox priest and I asked him if I could read his Bible. He knew the Bible very well but he did not keep what it says. I asked him about lots of verses and he told me that I could go astray reading the Bible. My mother had heard that I had repented during the earthquake and I started going to her church every Sunday. I got baptised that summer without my husband knowing. He did not even know I was going to church.

When they realised that I had given up drinking the persecution began. The mayor of the village called me in. I told him I had been baptised and he said my husband should divorce me and my father-in-law should disown me. I told him that I was willing to lose them all if I had to, but I was not willing to lose Jesus—I would not leave Him.

At the hospital where I worked as a nurse I had a good work record but hospital officials came to investigate me because of my faith with a view to sacking me. At work their attitude towards me changed completely. But when they and my husband's family treated me with hatred and rejection it was an opportunity to speak to them about Jesus.

One day my husband turned me out of the house and I had no-one with whom I could stay. My husband told me never to come back. I did return to him and he threatened me with an axe. His family would not tell me where my child was. All the time I knew that I had to keep witnessing to Jesus. I was looking everywhere for my child and my husband followed me and beat me so much my ears never recovered.

My husband thought that if he beat me enough he would beat the faith out of me. He used to drink a lot and my father-in-law was an alcoholic—in fact the whole family had problems with alcohol. I did not know this before I married into the family. They told me I was the anti-Christ.

I was eventually allowed back home again. It was Sunday evening and there was a knock on the door. It was my husband. He said he had heard a voice saying, 'Go and get her back.' He came for me and I went back to him. But when I got back my father-in-law tried to make me drink vodka and soon after my return my husband started to strangle me saying, 'either you renounce your faith or I am going to kill you.' I replied, 'I want the Lord and I want to stay married to you.' The next morning I got up at five and I took the Bible and I went to the Baptist church. The brothers there were praying for us and they were wondering how best to advise and help us. They took me home and spoke to my husband.

My father-in-law came to the hospital after me. He was furious with me and he slammed his fist down on the table and he would have killed me if he could, but it was a public place and he could not.

The whole village was against me. There was a bad family in the village who often stoned me on the way to work and they spat at me.

I had prayed so much for my husband. The church met in my mother's house and one day he started coming with me! When we got home from church on a certain day soon afterwards all our windows had been broken. My husband was very late getting home on one occasion and when he finally did his head was cut open and he had cuts everywhere. One of his brothers, who was also an Orthodox priest, and two other men had beat him up. They had axed his head at the back and he had lost consciousness. We went back that night to my parents. He was covered in blood. The pastor advised us to let the Lord take care of things and not to seek revenge. My mother's brother gave us a room to live in. My husband repented a year after we moved there.

Everyone asked us, 'Don't you miss your house?' I said I have a wonderful house waiting for me in heaven. My husband used to go back to his brothers in the village to tell them about the Lord. He has four brothers who are Orthodox priests now. My husband became a deacon in the church at Hîrtop. He had a heart to serve and he was very musical and directed the choir. My husband and I were full of zeal for the Lord even with lots of children. My husband couldn't wait to go to church.

We went through so many trials. The Lord told me to get up an hour earlier in the morning at 5 a.m. It wasn't so easy as we had cows to look after and work to do. I went to the church to pray and some of the sisters started to join me to pray. We brought all our needs to God and how we praised the Lord—that went on for twenty years. How I loved those times!

I told all my children about the Lord and how to live only for Him. My husband is with the Lord now. He worked so hard in building. They found out when he was working in Moscow that he had cancer but by then it was too late. I prayed for his healing but I was willing all the time for the Lord's will. He died during the operation in Chişinău but before the operation he was smiling knowing he might die and go to see the Lord. He said he knew where he was going and he had complete peace. He told the boys to serve the Lord in their youth. I am so thankful to God. It has not been easy but the Lord comforted me so much. I am so looking forward to seeing the Lord!

THEY USED TO CALL US BAD NAMES: BROTHER PETRU

Brother Petru was in his 40s and had vivid memories from childhood:

I was born into a Christian family. My father was a Baptist pastor in the village of Baroncea, Drochia. I was born in 1971 and I was converted when I was about 15 but I was not baptised until I was 21 as it was illegal before then. I was the ninth child in a family of eleven children. At school they used to call us bad names because of our faith and my parents also suffered much abuse too at the hand of unconverted relatives. They told them they had betrayed the true faith by not being Orthodox. Our church was a small, village church which was both conservative and strict but it was faithful to the doctrines of the Bible. There was a church choir and orchestra and I used to play the mandolin in church. It was all very interesting for us children. My father had a Bible which we read together as a family every evening. The song books I remember were all handwritten. Fellowship in the churches was much closer in those days. None of us in the church had a TV but we used to listen to Christian programmes on the radio every evening including messages from Earl Poysti. I think a lot of people used to listen to those broadcasts secretly.

I went to Technical School in Bălți in the north of Moldova and joined the church in Bălți from 1986 to 1989 which had about 1500 members then. It was a very active church and there were lots of young people and a large choir.

Despite the pressure to which individual believers, including children, were subject, a most daring plan was conceived by the church to address the severe lack of Bibles in the land. We will read more about this in the next two chapters.

5

INCREASED PRESSURE AND AN
INCREDIBLE LITERATURE WORK

BROTHER MIHAIL

I met brother Mihail in an unregistered church in the centre of the city. Time-keeping in Moldova has an elastic quality and I had waited outside the church for a very long time in freezing cold to see him. I was so glad when he arrived! We entered the empty church and he began to tell me his story. The events he described had a crucial place in his memory and he recounted them as though they were very recent events. He is still one of the leaders in the unregistered church. Here is his story :

In the early 1960s the Soviet letter to which churches were asked to subscribe, decreed that no children should be present in church services; State authorisation was needed for any baptisms; church finances were to be supervised by the State and visitors to the church had no right to preach but only the three men approved by the State could preach. To agree to all this you would have had to have betrayed all you held dear. The decree was an enormous blow to us. The authorities expected us to tell them how many attended our services, how many members there were and who and how many had been baptised.

Many of our young people in the 1970s had been expelled from places of higher education and they were asking me what to do. They often had to take on manual work. We had no right to type or print and we had no Bibles or songbooks. To purchase a Bible then cost the equivalent of 3000 MD lei [about £150].

We used to baptise in rivers during the night-time. I was baptised in 1976 when I was 22 years old. I had no Bible.

I was called into a work which involved the secret production of Christian literature. We often did not know the real names of those with whom we worked. It was mostly at night that we worked. Between 1972 and 1979 I was involved in this work and the location of the secret printing presses changed about four or five times during those years to avoid detection. We could disappear quickly.

During the years 1977–1979 we received 12 tons of Christian literature from Finland. Huge lorries carrying wood from Finland to Italy would come via Moldova and the literature was well hidden amongst the wood. Sometimes the border guards would bore through the wood to make sure there was no contraband on board, but they did not find any literature when I was involved in this ministry. Once the literature was through the border we were responsible for its distribution. It included Bibles, hymn books and children's Bibles. We distributed this literature very widely including to Central Asia, the Caucasus, the Ukraine, Kazakhstan, Tashkent and Alma Ata and Siberia. There were miracles getting this literature across the border. And Moldova was the hub of this distribution! We distributed 12 tons of literature for three years— a total of 36 tons during that time. Twelve brothers helped me who were willing to sacrifice themselves and their lives if necessary for this ministry. When I was arrested the charges included being an organiser of churches and a distributor of Christian literature.

During the interrogations I refused to confess guilt and I would not co-operate with the interrogators. They sent me to prison near the Baltic because they were worried about the influence I would potentially have in Siberia. From 1979 to 1984 I was in prison. During all this time the Lord kept me and led me in a special way and I was able to withstand all the humiliations and beatings and all the bad things that happened. Three days after my release from prison they called me back in and told me I had no right to be in the city.

I was ordained in 1987. We are fighting the good fight of faith and we need to fight a good warfare and keep the faith and a crown will be waiting for us. I have fought a good fight and I have kept the faith. We want to be His true children. As it says in 1 John, 'I have no greater joy than to hear that my children walk in the truth.' We have loved His Word and we have lived after this Word.

SISTER VERA KHOREV

Sister Vera Khorev elaborated on the later development of this literature work:

By 1984 large quantities of literature were still coming from Finland. The literature would be carried in big trucks sometimes which were sealed off, so they could not be searched as the seals could not be broken. Bibles would be hidden everywhere—very large quantities were needed. Whenever my husband was here he organised its distribution. It was all done very quickly and efficiently often at night in the forests. It was very well organised. Thousands of Bibles were distributed all over the Soviet Union. The literature needed to be distributed with the utmost speed.

Brothers began to be arrested for involvement in this ministry and were sometimes given sentences of 25 years or life.

I had read much about the secret printing presses of which Brother Mihail spoke but in the next chapter you will read how it actually became possible to visit the location of one such secret printing press!

6

A SECRET PRINTING PRESS!

*I*t was a grey day in December and driving, icy sleet was smashing against the windscreen of the minibus as we drove southwards through Moldova. Our dear sister Tatyana from the Ukraine was staying with us and we were journeying to a house she had not visited for 25 years! This was a place where she had served the Lord in a secret and dangerous ministry. Tatyana had been a member of one of the many teams in Soviet days who worked on secret printing presses. Such teams would remain incarcerated for months without going outside for fear of discovery. The families which housed them ran tremendous risks. If found they would be imprisoned and their children removed from their care. Those who worked on the printing presses, if found, were usually imprisoned for four years.

They were days in which there was a famine for the Word of God. The Scriptures were in direfully short supply and Christian literature of any kind was virtually unavailable apart from what was being smuggled across the border. So the leaders of the unregistered Baptist churches devised a plan to supply some of those needs and also to distribute information about Christians that were in prison so that the Lord's people could pray for them. It was ingeniously thought out and very bravely executed. Those not directly involved in this ministry took their part in supplying the needs of those who were. It was a most effective ministry in the hands of God.

> Organising the printing operation was a huge logistical task. Printing supplies and large quantities of paper could not be bought openly. Ink was home-made using bark, old tyres and scraps of metal. The air was often full of fumes from ink, turpentine and various chemicals. Sometimes we worked for 15 to 16 hours a day but the Lord strengthened us. The printing presses were constructed entirely out of parts borrowed from other machinery ranging from washing machines to bicycles. They could be fully dismantled and packed into suitcases to be moved to new location.
>
> *Russian Resurrection* Michael Rowe 1994

In common with many others at the time I had regularly prayed for those who worked on those secret printing presses. Whilst unaware of their precise locations and the names of the workers, we used to receive reasonably detailed information about their circumstances and photos and details of individuals who had been found by the KGB and arrested then imprisoned as a consequence of their involvement. But the work always seemed to find new servants to replace those who had been taken and the teams went on producing vast quantities of literature in seemingly impossible circumstances.

We drove up to a house on the edge of a village. Tatyana remembered the house though she had not seen it for many long years. A husband and wife in their 60s came out to greet us most welcomingly and ushered us into the warmth of their home. It was a single storey building. We sat round a long table and I could see that the husband was wiping tears away as he saw Tatyana again. [At this point I need to explain that the husband was in fact Brother Nicolae of Chapter 1 who had spent three years in prison and who subsequently lived as a fugitive in the forests to complete translation work he had been called to undertake—the Brother I called 'Mr Great-heart'].

His wife hurried to prepare a delicious meal. Precious fellowship in the Lord followed—it was one of those remarkable encounters I will never forget. I sat and listened and watched. Brother Nicolae was a big man with huge hands, grey curly hair, a lively face and a kind expression. He was a pastor in an unregistered church in that village.

The family later invited us to see the rooms in which the printing press team had worked. There was a part of the house that in those times had looked as though it was uninhabited. The windows were covered up with thick paper and the door to that part of the house had been left unpainted and neglected to draw attention away from it. They showed us how if the door handle was in a particular position it meant that it was possible to enter. To my amazement I learnt that even their children had not known about the presence of the team in their house! Neither had Brother Nicolae's father, who was a very frequent visitor to the house and a believer, any idea of what was going on in this home. Secrecy was absolutely paramount. Brother Nicolae's wife, Raia, related to us how she would go to different villages to do some of the shopping not to draw attention to the quantities of food she was purchasing. She would leave bags of produce at the door when the handle was in the right position which would be quickly taken into the secret dwelling. Tatyana showed us how they had covered up the inside of the outer door with blankets and thick materials to muffle the sounds and smells so as not to arouse suspicion. There were three rooms which the team of six used. One was used as a bedroom and a room where they rested from work; one was a laboratory where Tatyana explained there were strong chemical smells and the other was a room where the lettering was meticulously copied and typeset. And the team spent periods of three months shut up in this tiny little world.

Brother Nicolae and Sister Raia told us that each day they would carry a ton of water from their well—the printing work demanded huge quantities of water and this was before there were any taps in the house. Tatyana vividly recalled their great love and kindness as well as their great sacrifice and self-denial. Occasionally the workers would be taken individually to Chișinău to a believer's house in order to have a shower and wash their clothing. They did not exchange names with such people to limit the mutual risk if they were discovered. Tatyana shared with us that she had lost her job in the Ukraine because of her faith and for some while she had longed to join the printing press workers. She was asked shortly after losing her job if she would be willing to undertake such work. Having discussed it with her parents and having gained their agreement she started working far away from home in Moldova. How strange that we had come as it were full circle back to Moldova again after all those years!

Later that evening as we sat together with the large family chatting, I discovered that Brother Nicolae was a renowned Christian poet and an accomplished musician. We listened to the whole family singing as he played the balalaika and the guitar. It was a most wonderful evening and we rejoiced in the Saviour who had made such sweet fellowship possible. I was awed by the consecrated lives of those in whose presence I found myself and I remembered the hymn which says:

> *Love so amazing, so divine*
> *Demands my soul, my life my all.*

It was the most enormous and unexpected privilege for me to make that visit to a site of a former secret printing press that day and to meet those who at very great personal risk had served in that work.

So from times which were very difficult for the Lord's people in Moldova , we pass in the next chapter to the very beginnings of the awakening during the late 1980s.

II

PART TWO: THE AWAKENING
IN MOLDOVA

7

THE FIRST INDICATIONS OF A MOVE
OF GOD'S SPIRIT

hose I have spoken to indicated that the first lessening of pressure on the church from the State came towards the end of the 1980s. Gorbachev had become General Secretary of the Communist Party in 1985 and President of the Soviet Union in 1990. He introduced a policy of glasnost, meaning 'openness' and perestroika which referred to the reconstruction of the political and economic system of the Communist Party. Glasnost permitted criticism of Government officials and allowed the media freer dissemination of news and information. This allowed the churches to breathe a little easier for the first time in living memory.

One very significant event occurred in June 1988 when there was a celebration of 1000 years since the first Russian convert was baptised.

A MONTH OF PRAYER AND FASTING: SISTER NATALIA

Sister Natalia, my colleague in the Bible College, spoke of that time and the first indications of an awakening:

In the month of January 1987 our churches set aside the month for prayer and fasting both for the free expression of the Christian faith in the Soviet Union and for the release of Christians from prison. On March 1st that year, a month later, Gorbachev freed the Christian prisoners and announced freedom of expression of faith.

Towards the end of the month of prayer it was a Sunday and my father was preaching. The theme was prayer for the children of believing families. My father was preaching about Samuel and his family and the need for his children to believe for themselves. I understood clearly what my father was saying and there were tears in his eyes as he preached and the Holy Spirit was convicting me through those words. That day I repented and believed.

In 1988 I was baptised. Until then we used to baptise secretly but liberty was starting to come and I was baptised in the lake openly and lots of people came to the service. From 1988 we were able to start evangelising more freely. We celebrated the 1000th year anniversary of the first Christian baptisms in Kiev about then and we went to the Orthodox cathedral giving out Christian books and we preached the Word there.

Previously we had only one Bible for the whole family. But by 1988 books started to come in from Germany. Many unbelievers were asking for Christian literature. People were listening to the Christian broadcasts on the radio and had heard an announcement saying that if they wanted to receive a Bible they should write. We were given their addresses as well as big boxes of Bibles and we visited their homes to deliver the Bibles. Very many had so many questions about God when we visited. I can remember sometimes we would stay for four hours answering their questions. We went to the villages with literature also. There was an insatiable thirst after God everywhere. We used to give out books in the parks too and later heard about fruit from this work.

We were allowed to go to the prison for adolescents at Lipcani to evangelise. Our previous memories of prison had been visiting my father as a prisoner and now we were able to bring the Gospel to such places! Many had questions. We gave them our address and then after they were released they would come to see us. There were so many individual conversations about the Lord.

BROTHER GHILEȚCHI

Brother Ghilețchi (who is a pastor and a member of parliament), described the same period:

> The awakening began in 1988 under perestroika. In 1988 there was a celebration of 1000 years since the first Russian baptism and we used this as a great opportunity for outreach. Churches took the initiative and there were evangelistic outreaches everywhere. In the beginning Orthodox priests would even stand next to us when the Gospel was being preached—they were friendly to us in the beginning of this movement. We preached everywhere.

A THIRST FOR GOD: BROTHER LIVIU

I interviewed a dear older Christian, Brother Liviu, who was a doctor and would have been a member of the intelligentsia of his day. He described his sense of 'ennui' with the Communist system:

> During the 1980s few here realised what was happening over the border. But everyone here longed for change. We were weary with the Communist slogans and understood that we could not expect anything from the system. We also wanted to change in our own lives. It was as if there were an echo sounding through the people at the end of the 80s—it was a thirst for God. I was responsible for ideological education in the hospital where I was working and although I was supposed to teach about the non-

existence of God this was a subject I avoided as it touched something too near my heart. Many in our young generation then were disappointed in the regime and we saw no future for ourselves.

The way in which God worked in my life was in some ways typical for those of my generation. I had finished my medical training and I wanted to have a successful career as a surgeon. I was doing research for my doctorate. Yet deep in my inner being there was a lack of peace and profound dissatisfaction. My grandmother on my mother's side was a Christian from the Ukraine and I remembered going with her to her village church as a child. That was something that stood out in my childhood. The sense of dissatisfaction I felt grew and grew until I could find no pleasure in anything—not in my family, nor in my work. I became withdrawn. Only later I realised that God was working in my life through these things but I could not see it at the time.

A tragic event happened which brought things to a head. I had a Jewish patient and I operated on him. He did not get better—it was a complex case—and when he was dying he asked me a question, 'Doctor, is this life all there is?' That question and his voice pursued me day and night. It made me think so much and I read from literature and science trying to find an answer.

When I met with Christ in 1990 everything changed. My whole family repented, parents and children, and that was such a great joy…

A SCAR IN THE SOUL OF SO MANY: SISTER AURICA

Sister Aurica, a dear friend, was converted during the revival:

It was as though there were a scar in the soul of so many. There was great sadness in their souls but people began to pray. Before that they had been afraid to pray and they had no peace and were unable to forgive others. They had not been taught about the importance of forgiveness. People had been looking for justice anywhere apart from in God. They had suffered so much and they had no peace in their souls. If you cannot forgive there is no peace. Satan has no power to give peace—it is only the Lord who can do that. After 1990 there was a very great awakening and so many came to church and so many repented.

A PRICELESS POSSESSION: BROTHER ALEXANDRU

A friend of mine, Brother Alexandru, who is now a pastor and a lecturer in a Christian University and greatly used of God, shared the following experiences with me:

I came from an Orthodox context. I believed in God. My grandparents were Orthodox believers—they never denied the existence of God. At school I did well. I studied hard and my best friend there was the son of an Orthodox priest. He had access to crosses and icons but he never gave me a Bible. After school I went to Technical College and one of my class mates there too was the son of an Orthodox priest. I felt no inner conflict in the sense that I believed that God existed and my friends were the sons of priests. At College we had to attend compulsory lectures on 'scientific atheism.' These strengthened my faith! I realised that atheism had no solid, theoretical basis as all the arguments they used were not arguments against the existence of God but 99% of their arguments were about priests and churches which had compromised the truth by immorality or a lack of love. The response in my heart was that it confirmed that people are sinners which I already believed. They argued that in Tsarist times the church had been used as a means to subjugate the people and that the Soviet Union had freed us from that bondage. I agreed that priests had sometimes served the State not the Lord but that did not mean that there was no God. There was no logical connection that led to this conclusion. Their observations were correct but their conclusions were wrong.

In 1988 I was called up to the Soviet Army when I was 19 years old and I was in the army until I was 21. By this time I had not met a single Protestant Christian but I believed in God in my heart. After about ten months I received a parcel from my mother which had not been opened by the authorities. It contained a New Testament and Psalms and had an orange cover and it said it was printed in Germany—it did not look like a Bible from the outside. My mother had been converted in 1988 at the Bethel Church. I started to read the Bible my mother had sent me. I used to keep it inside my jacket next to my military card. God started to speak to me when I was reading it. At first I was careful when I read it but after a year or so I was more open about reading it. My mother wrote to me about how to pray, what repentance meant and how to find peace with God. She listened to the preaching and she would write to me about what she had learnt. She never wrote about the Baptists—she wrote about Christ and about the Cross and about eternity. I started to pray seriously when I was in the army. I was already praying but now it was different. I realised that although I believed in God I had not understood the meaning of the Cross.

In the Soviet Army sometimes you would be allowed a day off to go into town as a reward for good behaviour. You were allowed time off in town from 9 a.m. to 9 p.m. on a Sunday. You had to wear army uniform and you were not allowed to drink alcohol. My faith was growing in understanding. I had my New Testament and Psalms in my pocket and I went to church and I showed it to the priest as I thought I could trust him. I was brought up to esteem and respect such men. In those days the priests had a respect for soldiers. They understood something of our situation and they were kind to us. I took out my New Testament. His first question was where did I get it from and he had an amazed look on his face, particularly when he discovered it also contained the

Psalms. I told him someone had given it to me as a present. He said to me, 'Son, read this book and do everything that it says.' He was sincere and wise in his answers. To possess a Bible then was to have a priceless possession. He increased my desire to read this Word and he rejoiced for me and with me. So today I say that through the blessing of an Orthodox priest I became a Baptist pastor!

My spiritual awakening began then. I began sharing my faith with my colleagues there in the army. I used to see Muslim soldiers praying secretly before their meals and giving thanks for the food. In the army I was friendly with the son of a lecturer on atheism. He tolerated my faith and tried to explain to me about the Holy Trinity. So an atheist had told his son what the Holy Trinity meant and his son was telling me! God can use any context He is so wonderful!

I had some opportunities to speak publicly about the rights of soldiers. This was my first experience of speaking to large numbers in public and God used this to train me too. The message changed afterwards from the rights of soldiers to the salvation of souls. In all these ways God was forming my Christian character and preparing me for preaching.

In the same year that I left the army I repented publicly and was baptised at Bethel Church. From 1988 a great awakening started in our country. What I saw was a great opening for the Gospel and a great desire for God.

From those early stirrings during the latter years of the 1980s the Holy Spirit worked in such a way in Moldova in the 1990s that believers describe in the following chapter how they entered the full flood tide of revival.

8

THE FULL FLOOD

*A*ll the people I spoke to agreed that the awakening started in 1988 to 1989. Despite many having prayed for a time of refreshing from the Lord, it came suddenly and unexpectedly. Many said that the church had been completely unprepared for such a move of the Spirit of God. As I listened to one and another relating the events of those times I was thrilled to hear of the power and mercy of God in visiting Moldova.

BROTHER SERGHEI

Brother Serghei is in his 40s and is a pastor and a lecturer in theology at the Christian University. I have known him for years. He trained in theology in Oradea, Romania and returned to Moldova to teach others. This was his story:

> I was born into a family of Baptist believers but our earliest roots were Orthodox. My grandfather was an Orthodox priest. My mother was converted through listening secretly to the Gospel being preached on the radio and then my father was saved. Both my parents became Christians before I was born.

I was Bulgarian by background so I went to Tiraspol University in Transnistria as I didn't know Romanian. There were some lads there who used drugs and I began to use them too and sometimes I stole. My father found out about my drug use and sent me to live with a pastor and his family there but I continued to use drugs. One day 1000 roubles went missing from the pastor's family and they asked me if I had stolen the money. This was a very large sum in those days. His question had the most enormous effect on me—that he could think I could do such a thing! I decided to commit suicide by drowning in the River Nistru and I got on the bus to go there. I wanted to find a part of the river where there would not be people around. But the bus took ages to get anywhere near the river and when I eventually got to the river bank I no longer wanted to drown myself.

I was 17 years old and a sceptic and an atheist. A female colleague gave me a copy of *Mere Christianity* by C S Lewis in Russian. There was a chapter in the book about pride and I realised that pride was my biggest problem. I was converted at Tiraspol through some Christian colleagues in the Technical College.

In May 1992 the war was going on in Tiraspol so I stayed there and began work there. It was not possible to leave because of the war. [Please see the Timeline at the beginning of the book for an explanation of this civil war]. So I was in Transnistria at the time of the awakening.

Things were much stricter there and we were not allowed to use the stadiums for evangelism. Nevertheless we used the churches for evangelism and a great number of people repented even as the war was going on outside. In the church in Tiraspol where I was there would be tank explosions outside and the church would be full and the whole congregation would be on their knees. I was the church watchman during that time! Even when there were no services due to take place people flooded into the churches. We held services every single evening and the church was always full to bursting. There was a *great* hunger for God everywhere. People would take tracts without any prompting and they had so many questions. A brother would start preaching at a trolley bus stop or anywhere and a crowd would quickly gather to listen. This lasted from about 1990 to 1997. We were baptising 50 people at a time. Our parents had prayed for such a revival. They had lived through times when Christians had suffered much for Christ. They were used to fines and imprisonments.

PASTOR NICOLAE

I spoke to another pastor called Nicolae, also in his forties. As he related the events of those years he became animated by what he was describing and told me he could have spent many hours recalling those times. He has recently been appointed as Bishop of the Baptist Union in Moldova.

The period from 1990 to 2000 was a very special time. Often I would walk six kilometres to church to preach the Gospel and would talk to everyone along the way about the Lord. On the main street, Ștefan Cel Mare, in about 1995 as soon as you started preaching a crowd would gather. Everyone wanted to listen. They were starving to hear the Word of God.

A GREAT WAVE OF OPPORTUNITY

Pastor Alexandru (the brother who became a Baptist pastor through the blessing of an Orthodox priest!) said:

During the 1990s very many were coming to faith. There were so many that they couldn't fit into the churches—they would be at the windows, in the courtyard—the churches were packed. The Lord put it on the brothers' hearts to plant churches in every sector of Chișinău. We only learnt the term, 'church planting' afterwards, then we had no adequate vocabulary for what the Holy Spirit was doing.

Many pastors understood what the Lord was doing. We need to grasp when the Spirit begins to move and follow His leading. We needed new direction for the work because of the way the Holy Spirit was working. He works where He wills. Some of the unregistered churches did not always use the time when the Lord began to move in power but the registered churches did use those opportunities. It is the Lord Himself who opens doors—our task is to go through them. We were united in our desire to evangelise. There was a great wave of opportunity when the Holy Spirit was working in power and we needed to take advantage of that time that the Lord gave us when so many were calling on the Lord. We need to go at the movement of the Spirit. Sometimes obstacles from the past can damage the present and ruin the future. I have never been disappointed in God. Governments come and go but our relationship with Jesus endures.

Pastor Grigore said:

In the 1990s there was an awakening across the land and the stadiums would be full for preaching services. Our prayer houses were full too and so many repented then. God wanted us to use that time. Maybe we did not use it to its full—nobody knew how long it would last. It was like the angel in the New Testament troubling the waters and it was the time for us to act.

Brother Petru remembered:

We made our own tracts to give to people. What I remember about those years in the 90s is that so many people were hungry for God. We used to give them slips of paper to write details about their names and addresses. On the back of the paper it asked if they wanted a visit from a pastor. Most of them did and they had so many questions about God when we visited them! This movement of God's Spirit lasted powerfully until about 1997. We would preach everywhere and there was a lot of street evangelism. It was no problem to approach anyone and they would stop and talk to you. Everyone was open to talk about the Gospel and in schools they were happy for us to preach. We even had opportunities to preach in the Army Base and to the Special Forces. And they listened. Everyone wanted to hear what we preached.

GOD'S TIME TO WORK

A pastor, Brother Serghei, shared:

After 1990 a people who had denied the existence of God were desperate to hear about Him! Do you see what is impossible with men is possible with God! The generation that preceded us had prayed—oh how they had prayed! God opened the doors in a way we never expected. We had prayed but we could not believe it when it happened like the church in Jerusalem praying for Peter's release and then not believing it when he was knocking at the door. We were not prepared. But God has His time to work. God worked in such a way that eighteen churches were planted from our one church, Bethel. Our brothers here who were mature in the Lord realised that the liberty would not last and they encouraged the churches to make every effort to preach the Gospel to as many as possible in this time of freedom. There were no obstacles to preaching and evangelism. And the Spirit came. Now we have so many churches because of that time. There were big evangelistic meetings in the 1990s with preachers like Sami Tipet and Victor Gam. We were all involved in these meetings. Our hearts were burning for God—my heart is still burning for Him. God allowed this liberty and we worked as those on fire for

God. We preached everywhere, in parks, on the street, in schools, and everywhere people repented. They listened to the Word and the Holy Spirit was at work. After people repented we organised courses to teach them further. We needed to disciple them then. The churches multiplied! I believed that the Lord would bring an awakening. The church knew that such an awakening would happen. Many did not live to see it. It was the Lord's work.

A VOICE FROM SIBERIA

An elderly pastor, Andrei, who had spent years in Siberia told me:

It is the Lord from who all blessings come and they come from the Lord in His time. Everything is according to His will. I can remember some brothers saying in the 1970s that a time would come when the Gospel would be preached in stadiums and on the streets here. That was at a time when you could not even sing a Christian song to yourself outside. But it happened! We preached everywhere—in stadiums, on the streets, in the Casa de Cultură [The Communist equivalent of a community/arts centre].

THE AWAKENING IN BETHEL

Bethel Church was the only registered church open in Chișinău at the time when the Soviet Union fell. It is a huge building, constructed by the members in a time of very considerable difficulty under the Communists. [The story of the building of this church is related in my first book *With God All Things Are Possible*].

Talking of what happened in the Bethel Church in Chișinău, Pastor Dumitru said:

The time of the awakening in Bethel was a very special time. There was not standing room in the church during the services (a church building holding about 3000 people). The church was full to bursting and the church already had about 1500 members. The pastors were baptising over 100 people at a time. For the first time we could talk publicly about God and the people were so thirsty to hear about Him! The preaching at the time was simple. You could not say that there were deep, profound expositions of the Word but so many were literally starving to know the Lord and the Christians were longing to be involved in serving the Lord –they were so on fire to serve the Lord. The Holy Spirit convicted deeply of sin.

So many pastors and believers when they spoke with me used the word 'fire' for the work that the Lord had done in their hearts and in the churches. There were many extraordinary conversions during the revival.

In the next chapter we will read of a Mafia boss who came to Christ at that time.

9

A MAFIA BOSS

*T*he awakening saw many unusual conversions of which the following accounts are a very small number of examples.

VALERA

One of the men I interviewed was 52 years old. I had known him for many years as a Christian worker and a wonderful expositor of the Word of God. His stature is large, one of my friends has said that he looked like a Russian bear and I knew that he had a black belt in judo. He is the kind of person that you would naturally hold in awe. But as he started to recount the story of his conversion I was amazed. I had had no idea that the person I thought I knew quite well had been converted from mafia stock! This is his story and his name is Valera.

> I was converted in 1995 during the revival. The revival had started at the end of the 1980s. Our family are from Truşeni and my grandfather on my father's side was a Christian. He was one

of the founder members of the church in our village. He died when he was only in his early 30s.

Our family was a disaster. My father had a very bad reputation in the village and people did not want anything to do with him. My childhood was not easy. My father had a lot of money but he never gave my mother any money and she had to work in three different jobs. We loved our mother though. My father used to hit her a lot.

I WANTED TO TRAVEL THE WORLD

When I was in Class 5 I left the village to go to Chișinău to study sports. I wanted to travel the world and become a great sportsman. I was an expert in judo and the martial arts and I travelled a lot in the former Soviet Union through this means. Then I realised that if I went to a merchant navy school I could travel. So in 1981 I went to Karelia in Russia to attend such a school. I specialised in the transport of goods and I learnt how to steer a ship. There would even have been opportunities to travel outside the Soviet Union. However, during my last year of training I beat up three policemen and there was a chance that I would be sent to prison. I inherited many character traits from my father. They arrested me and I was locked up. There was a lady prosecutor who agreed that there were provocations on both sides. She told me that if I agreed to go into the Soviet Army she would help me to avoid a prison sentence. I agreed to go. I was 18 then.

I loved fighting. I wanted to fight in Afghanistan. I did my best to get into the Special Forces. There were six months of training for the Special Forces and it was very demanding. I got in and I was sent to Afghanistan. I was a very tough, cruel man and I loved fighting in Afghanistan. War is a drug. You want more and more. I enjoyed having a gun in my hand—you can imagine what was happening in my heart. Often I could have been killed. Our helicopter crashed and I survived because God kept me. God had a plan because it was impossible to survive that sort of crash. We were all wounded. When I had got into the helicopter I took my weapons and ammunition and rucksack off which was strictly forbidden. There was lots of ammunition and weapons in the helicopter. When the crash happened I was thrown under the weapons and the helicopter was turning over and over and I was thinking we were dead already. If I had had my weapons and ammunition on I would never have got out of there. All the doors were blocked apart from a very small skylight window above me. I have no idea how I got out of there but I did. Our soldiers came and broke the windows and got us all out. Then the helicopter exploded. It was His hand alone! I used to carry an amulet with me to save me but it disappeared during that crash and I never used it again. I was sorry at the time to have lost it but when I came to Jesus I understood that it was better to have lost it.

I returned home from Afghanistan and began drinking very heavily. I had been hit on the head often in the war through explosions and being hit. I had travelled all over Afghanistan. At night I had terrible nightmares and always dreamt that I was fighting. Most of the veterans from Afghanistan suffered like this. My mother was afraid of what I had become. I drowned myself in alcohol.

I wanted to change and find peace but peace eluded me. I got involved in a Mafia gang and I began to associate with some seriously bad people. I took part in lots of bad things such as theft and beating up people. I loved money but I could not cope with authority. People feared me because I was very aggressive. They wanted nothing to do with me. That lasted until the 1990s. I was a member of the most renowned Mafia gang in Moldova and farther afield.

At the beginning of the 1990s many of us Mafia began to work with businessmen who were crooks. Anyone with money feared the Mafia because we knew them all. I acquired an enormous amount of money very quickly. I knew politicians, bank managers and deans of the university. It seemed to me that I was doing very well. But I thought about building an orphanage or an old people's home because my past bothered me and I wanted to atone for my past sins.

My cousins were believers and they used to come to see me but they didn't say anything to me about God apart from one of them. They were older than me. In the army I had wanted to join the KGB but I was not allowed to because I had relatives who were converted.

I LOST EVERYTHING

By 1995 the business was doing very well and I told the Executive Director that we would never need to borrow money again. A week later I had lost everything. Then I got into terrible debt. I realised how cruel the men were with whom I had been dealing. But I was not afraid of anyone. I had even had a link with Chechnya in the past.

Someone high up lent me a large amount of money and I did not want to give it back so a file was opened on me and I was arrested and then released after a week. I could have faced a life sentence or the death sentence but at that very time the Penal Code changed and in a month without any penal consequences I was free again.

THE BOOK OF MOSES

At the time I was living with a woman who was a prostitute. She gave me a book to read and told me it might help me. Its title was *The Book of Moses*. It was in Russian and I could see my name which attracted my interest. [Brother Valera's family name means 'Moses']. I wanted to know who this Moses was who wrote this book. (It was the Pentateuch). I started reading through curiosity about the name and I decided to read it all. I was amazed. It was all about me. It was all speaking about me. I didn't know that there was such a thing as the Bible. I got to Exodus and read about Moses when he was taken out of the water. When I was about 2 years old I nearly died in a flooded hole. I remember that I couldn't get out even though my brothers and sisters were not far away. My grandmother came and got me out. When I read that Moses was rescued from water I thought, 'That's me!' Everywhere I read in this book I saw me. It made me feel special because the person who wrote it knew me. I thought it was supernatural that someone knew all about me. My sins overwhelmed me the more I read. And hell became very real to me too. But it was as if there was Someone behind me all the time telling me that I had to go on reading even though I was afraid.

I managed to get hold of an Old Testament after that and reading through it I realised that my good works, such as wanting to start an orphanage would never ever save me. I started to see a Person who would come to save us when I was reading the Prophets. About this time my interest in playing cards and gambling waned. I was on my own and for the first time I knelt down and I started to cry. That was the first time I really prayed.

That autumn I started to read the New Testament (purchased on the black market for a large sum) and I met Jesus and I understood very clearly that He is the Lamb of God. I saw Him in all His beauty and I understood Him in the context of all the sacrifices of the Old Testament. But I was reluctant to change and I thought I would wait to repent until I was to see Him coming on the clouds of glory.

Soon after that I got into a bad conflict and they beat me up terribly. There were about twenty of them and they beat me up as if they were kicking a football around. Even as they were beating me up I told the Lord that I would serve Him until the end of my life. I was so badly injured after that that I was in bed for two weeks. I began to plan vengeance on them all but I heard a mild voice saying, 'Do you think what you are planning is good?' 'Do you really think you can leave it to the last minute to repent?' I realised that it was a miracle that I was still alive. I said to the Lord, 'Yes Lord, I give myself to You'.

It was 1995 and I was 30 years old. I decided to look for a church. A relative asked me for a lift to the 'Izvorul Vieții' [Fountain of Life] Church. I wondered what kind of church it was and I went back there to see one evening. It was dark and cold I remember and I was reading the church notice board when I heard a voice, 'What do you want here?' I thought it was the devil trying to dissuade me but I discovered it was the night-watchman! He told me the next meeting was on Friday. So off I went to that church on the Friday dressed up in my mafia garb with my head down not looking at anyone. I kept my head down for the whole service with no eye contact with anyone. It seemed to me that the pastor was talking all about me when he was preaching. I was still using drugs then.

FOUND OF GOD

But I did not have real peace yet and one day after the evening service I went to see the Pastor whose name was Belev and told him about this. He said, 'Don't you think God has forgiven you?' We sat down in the vestry and he read to me the account of the crucifixion and the two thieves crucified with Jesus. As he was reading the Lord had powerful dealings with me and all my life passed before me like lightning. And I knelt and prayed, 'Lord if you have forgiven that thief please forgive me too!' And I received a peace that truly passes understanding. I went home that evening as though I was flying and I was singing all the way. It was such an extraordinary experience. After that I never used drugs or cigarettes or alcohol again. I went to see my former mafia colleagues including all of those who had beaten me up and I asked each for forgiveness and told them that I had nothing at all against them. I forgave the very worst of them. God changed my whole attitude and I forgave all my enemies. I have no enemies now. This was all only because of Jesus.

I am so thankful for the brothers in the church who cared for me in the 1990s and for Pastor Belev because he trusted me. Mafia lads started coming to church then and brother Vasile Filat helped us a lot too and taught us the Scriptures. God transformed my life through all this.

During the 1990s it was very easy to reach people's hearts with the Gospel. We were all so active during those years. God gave me a teaching gift and I was able to equip people with the Word of God including in Central Asia. That was His work. I formed many teams of Bible teachers in post-Soviet States. During the awakening we could evangelise absolutely anywhere including on the streets and people came flooding into the churches. God visited us.

When I look back at all I have come through, including the most terrible things, I understand now that it was all somehow in His plan. The devil did everything possible to destroy me but God's grace was greater in drawing me. The devil was put to shame again and again. I understood that Christ was modelling me and making me like Him. I learned to submit and to forgive. God gave me a family too and we get through things together. I have a wonderful wife who knows how to encourage and we rejoice in the children. We rejoice that we can speak of Him and see the miracles he does. He will work everything out for us.

In the next chapter, we will read of the conversion of three more people during the revival. The first man, who is now a pastor, served a six year prison sentence for crime in his youth, was converted and later became the Dean of a Theology Faculty! Then follows the story of a KGB officer and his wife who were converted. Lastly, I tell the story of a friend of mine from the north of Russia who came to Moldova as a child with her parents and was converted at the baptism of her husband.

A CONVICT IS CONVERTED; HE BECAME A DEAN OF THEOLOGY!

*B*rother Dumitru agreed to be interviewed. I had known him for a number of years as a pastor and as the Head of Theology in the Christian University where I taught. The story of his conversion took me by surprise!

I was born in the south of the Ukraine in a Romanian speaking village. There was an evangelical church there and an Orthodox church but at that time there was a powerful atheistic influence in schools and society.

In our village all the parents told the children to make every effort to learn well at school. This was true even for Christian families like ours where there was no prospect that the children could go on to higher education. There was atheistic pressure at school. The church did not allow the children to undertake extra-curricular activities at school and some of those activities would have been good. Ours was a Pentecostal church in the village with about 500 members and there were other churches. There were a lot of believers in our village. We used to ask our parents why some things were forbidden and the legalism alienated some young people from church. Legalism can lead young people to question everything and to try to break all the limits imposed. [By legalism Brother Dumitru is referring to church traditions born out of habit without any biblical basis].

At the age of 17 I decided to give up church and to live without God. I was very much under the influence of my friends at the time. I was studying tele-communications in Chișinău and I committed a crime which resulted in a six year prison sentence. My term of imprisonment commenced in 1987 when I was 22 years old. It was only when I was serving a long sentence in prison that I began to see things clearly and I realised that my parents had always been alongside me. They travelled the long distance from the Ukraine to see me and to attend my trials which were sometimes deferred. I saw who my real friends were —my parents. They did not judge me but kept on loving me as they always had. They wanted to support me in everything. No-one expected the sentence to be as long as six years but it was good in the sense that it made me think about so many things. I remembered how my father used to read the Bible to me as a child and how we used to go to church. I remembered it all.

I repented on 20th December 1987 in prison. I was the only Christian in the prison then but the change inside me was real and profound. In 1990 the first Christians visited the prison and the first Bibles came into the prison. (I had one previously but had to hide it). Also in 1990 a service started taking place in the prison in Cricova and on 15th July 1990 I was baptised in the prison. I got married in prison and about 1000 prisoners came to the wedding service and there was a choir from Bethel Church and an orchestra!

In the autumn of 1991 I was transferred to a semi-open prison at Basarabeasca and I learnt construction and started working in building. (I can still do all our repairs!) My wife moved there and we lived in a rented place near the prison. My wife was working in a factory and my eldest daughter was born during that time.

I became a member of Bethel Church and they encouraged me

to preach in the prison and in the church. When I left prison I attended the Mission Bible School which started at Bethel and then I was sent to St Petersburg to study theology. We came back from St Petersburg in 1996 by which time we had three children.

Ever since I was converted it was crucial for me to know the Lord's guidance in my life. I wanted my children to see this as well and they experienced it in our family life—how the Lord has led us and continues to lead us. I knew the clear call of God to serve here in Moldova. God invested so much in me and I was able to do two Master's degrees and a doctorate. It would have been incorrect not to have obeyed Him in the place of my service. I have never sought to leave. It is very important to be where the Lord wants you. There you have peace and the Lord is with you even if you pass through difficulties. I am fulfilled here and this is where my calling is. There is so much to do. There is no temptation for me to leave.

A KGB OFFICER IS FOUND OF CHRIST—AND HIS WIFE FOLLOWS

I have known Sister Aurica and her husband, Ghena, for a number of years. All the time I have known them they have been Christians actively involved in the Lord's service, both with the Gideons and reaching out to families who have children with disabilities. They have two sons, one of whom has a disability and uses a wheelchair. I had no idea about Ghena's background once again until speaking to them of their conversion. In Sister Aurica's words:

I am from a Christian family and I had always heard about God. I married Ghena who was not a Christian when I was 18. I was not converted then. Ghena didn't know anything about Christians previously but he had worked with a Christian once whose life had impressed him. And then he met my family and they were all

Christians and he used to go to church with us. I can remember the first time he came to church with us he said to me, 'If God exists, He is here.' Ghena had a very good job working for the KGB as a leading officer and he was responsible for communications to Moscow. No-one believed in God in the circles in which he worked.

My aunt suggested that we be married in her Baptist church. She wrote a letter to the pastor asking for permission for us to be married there even though we were not Christians at the time. They agreed and they even laid hands on us during the marriage service.

Ghena was the first of us to be converted, at Easter time in Bethel Church. We went to the church but I stayed in the car with the two children. After about two hours he came out of the church and I noticed straight away that his face was white. I looked at him and became concerned and asked him what had happened. He told me that there had been a call to repentance during the service and he had rushed out to the front of the church and fell to the floor in tears. It was 1996. From that day onwards Ghena followed the Lord and he never smoked or drank again. If the Holy Spirit touches a man nothing can separate us from God. People say that they are not able to change but when the Holy Spirit is working in power He can do anything.

Ghena had problems with the KGB after his conversion. They stopped sending him to Moscow when they discovered that he was going to church.

I [Aurica] was not baptised until 2002 which was long after my husband was converted and baptised. I wanted to see how real the change was in Ghena's life. I was converted after seeing my husband's changed life. Now we do everything through prayer. We have been together for 28 years now. Even when difficult things happen in our family we kneel and pray and we go on.

FROM THE FAR NORTH

Sister Lena is one of my dear friends. She and her husband, Slava, have a son, Vasya, who has autism, and a daughter Nastea. Lena is now in her 50s and like many of her generation came to Moldova with her parents who were sent to work in this Soviet outpost as part of the Russification of the Soviet Republics. Such immigrants were generally granted privileged accommodation and salaries.

I was born in the north of Russia near the border with China in the town of Belogorsk. It was very cold in winter and very hot in the summer. I lived there from 1960 to 1969. I remember the house, the cow, the garden and my school. It was a very happy time. My brother had been born in 1956. In 1969 we moved to Moldova. My father was in the military and he was sent there to guard the borders.

I did not come from a Christian family though my father told me that he used to sing in an Orthodox choir as a child. My mother kept some Christian festivals but did not go to church. They spoke very little of God. I discovered later that my mother had given copies of the Lord's Prayer and the ten commandments to all her work colleagues. There was only one believer at my mother's workplace.

I enjoyed school. I went to college and then to university to study economics and I graduated with the highest marks. I never heard anything about God and I never thought about God. I was a very patriotic young person, proud of the USSR and a very active Komsomolist. I wore the Komsomol insignia with genuine pride.

My father died when I was 20 years old. I had become friendly with a young man who served in the army in Afghanistan. He came back in 1981 when my father died. My heart broke when my father died. I so needed support and six months later this young man proposed to me and I married him. I gave birth to Nastea but my husband left me for another woman. It was such a difficult time for me. I brought up Nastea on my own but I was always in deep, emotional pain.

When I was 27 years old I learnt from my mother that I had not been baptised as a child and so I went to the Orthodox church. I thought my life would be easier and I would be happier if I were baptised. The priest asked me why I had come. I told him quite sincerely that my soul needed this act of baptism. My life was morally in a bad way at the time.

I was 32 years old when I met Slava in a group of friends. I thought this man would look after me and my daughter. I decided to accept him. About the time when Nastea started school the Gideons began their work and she brought me a Gideon New Testament from her school. I used to keep it in my bag all the time but without reading it. I read only the verses they suggest you use in various situations when you need help. I thought this book helped me. I wanted to take it everywhere with me.

Slava and his mother started going to Bethel Church. In 1993 our son Vasya was born. Slava's mother kept phoning me up and inviting me to church and telling me that I needed to repent. Slava would come home from church saying, 'We must repent, we must repent!' I used to tell him to leave me in peace. I did not understand what he wanted of me. Then Slava was converted and he invited me to his baptismal service. I only went to observe what was going on, I had no other intention. Slava's mother had died about a month before his baptism. When they called us to repentance I went forward and I said to the Lord, 'I can't live like this anymore.' Vasya was about six years old at the time. In January 2000 I was baptised. At least twenty others were baptised with me.

There were very many who were converted in the same year that I was and today many of them are serving the Lord faithfully as pastors. There was a great seeking after God in those years. My heart was burning to serve God. I was very active in the Gideons and we used to work in the hospitals giving out New Testaments and speaking to patients and staff about the Lord. I remember we used to speak to people everywhere about the Lord. We were on fire for God—it was the time of our first love for the Saviour. I always wanted to do more to serve Him. I grew much spiritually through the Gideons. They really helped me. There were very good leaders in the group and they used to ask us challenging, formative questions. They realised that we needed to be strong in the Word if we were giving out this Word.

Sister Lena and her husband Brother Slava have been involved in a most fruitful work amongst families with children with disabilities for a number of years. So from an atheistic, Communist party background they were converted and drawn into the Lord's most wonderful service.

In the next chapter we will read the story of two women who were converted during this revival – one from a village and another from the city.

'A MOVEMENT OF GOD IN OUR VILLAGE'

$\mathcal{S}$ ister Lidia is from a village in the north of Moldova and worked as an English teacher for years. She is in her 60s now and she keeps a cow which she takes up to pasture each day. We sometimes chat on a bench waiting for the cows to be brought down from the pasture in the evenings. Sister Lidia loves to speak about what the Lord has done for her. The revival affected the whole of Moldova. Far away from the capital in the north of the country the same all powerful Holy Spirit was moving in many hearts.

Here then is the story Sister Lidia, whose heart the Lord opened, recounted :

I was born in Sofia and live in my parents' old house. My parents were from an Orthodox background but they were converted before I was. One day in 1982 my mother went to a funeral. There were believers at this funeral. She came home with such a radiant joy and she kept telling us that the funeral was beautiful. I could not understand it at all. How could you say that a funeral was beautiful? She said the singing was wonderful. My mother could not stop talking about what she had seen and heard at the funeral.

The next day she was looking after my son Victor and carrying on with her normal jobs but that day she died. She was 70 years old. I am sure she had become the Lord's—only the Lord could give her such joy. Her heart had been prepared.

After my mother's death my father was converted. He was 77 years old. He was not an alcoholic but he liked a drink and smoked. After he repented there was the most amazing change in him. The Lord completely transformed him. He was so thankful for everything! I can remember his words of thankfulness to me. I didn't realise that it was the power of the Lord Jesus that had changed him totally. I wish my mother had seen it. I know that my parents are with the Lord.

In 1993 I went to do a two week course in Chișinău. I was returning to the station to get the train home with some work colleagues when a young man spoke to me there. I can still remember what he said to me. He said, 'Your sins are black like coal but the blood of Jesus can make you as white as snow. If you come to Him, He will make you clean and then you must go and turn from your sin.' My colleagues told me not to listen to him. I went with them but this young man's words had such a powerful effect on me! His loving attitude and his words and the fact that he said he would pray for me really struck me.

In 1995 my son Victor became friendly with a group of Christians in our village with whom he used to play football. He was very impressed by their behaviour and the fact that they did not use bad language. On Sundays he used to disappear and did not say where he was going. Eventually I spoke to a lady named Eugenia, in whose house these young people were meeting. I asked her what Victor was involved with. She said, 'We pray and praise and sing to the Lord.' I did not understand. One day Victor came home and told us he had repented. We did not understand the words. What struck me profoundly was that there was such a change in him! He became much more reliable and honest and asked our forgiveness if he had done something wrong. At school

86

the teachers said he had improved a lot. In my heart I was glad about the change in him. Victor used to read the Bible regularly and I could see that the power of God was in him.

One New Year we were all going to a masked ball. I was upset that Victor would not agree to go with us. He was very strong in the Lord. He said, 'The Lord Jesus gives me so much joy those things are rubbish in comparison for me.' To me it was all very odd .

My son Andrei married in 1996. By this time we realised that Victor's Christian friends were good people. My son and two of his Christian friends came to the wedding. They sang two Christian songs and Victor preached for the first time. [Today Victor is a pastor in Romania]. This was all completely unexpected and it was like a bomb had fallen at the wedding! His brother Andrei and the guests were all shocked.

In 1997 Victor was baptised. At that time there was a real movement of God in our village. Victor was baptised in the lake and 22 young people were baptised with him that day. So many young people were coming to the Lord at that time.

I can remember a huge crowd of young people coming to sing carols at our gate one Christmas. I woke to the sound of these wonderful voices and I went out to see them with my heart full of joy.

I started going to the church and I found such fulfilment there. I had started reading the Bible a long time before this and gradually as I was reading, God exposed my sin to me and I realised I was a sinner. I felt black with sin and unworthy. Victor had told me that was good. I understood more and more in the Bible and I loved reading it. It became a wonderful treasure to me.

Sometimes I have bad pain but I'm not afraid of death. I'm going home to the Lord. Once I fell downstairs and I felt His arms upholding me—I felt His arms! I could easily have died but He kept me.

'I ONLY KNEW I NEEDED FORGIVENESS'

Sister Tamara is another very dear friend and I have been deeply thankful for her prayers for me year after year. Her life has been hard. She is in her 60's now and has a son but also a daughter who is in her 20's, Olga, who has Down's syndrome. Her husband used to be a journalist. Praise, thankfulness and prayerfulness characterise her life.

I am from a very strict Orthodox family. I used to go to church regularly with my mother and we held the four major fasts each year. But it was always as though something was missing. As time went by I grew less interested in the church. I didn't understand what it was all about. I left feeling as empty as when I went there. Eventually a sense of disgust for these things grew in me—it all seemed such empty form. After Olga was born in 1992 I went to the Sfânta Maria Church in Chişinău and I took communion. I didn't understand any of it and that was the end of it for me. I said to myself, 'I'm never coming here again, it's a waste of time.' I was discouraged by all of it. People were making a noise and talking when the priest was reading.

A friend of my mother's said that if I learnt the Lord's Prayer and the Creed and Psalm 51 by heart I would be saved. I heard this and began to learn them by heart. It was about 1990 and I was 29 years old. I heard that there were Bibles—before that there weren't any. I started to look for a Bible. A colleague at work said that she had a Bible from her grandmother. I asked for a loan of the Bible for two weeks and I started to copy the Bible by hand. I didn't sleep much at night and continued the second day and night but by the third day I was so tired I thought it was impossible to write it all out by hand. The Lord saw my interest. My husband phoned one day from Chişinău to tell me he had a Bible! He came home with a New Testament. He had gone to a press conference and the Gideons had given all the journalists a Bible. I gave my friend her Bible back.

I began to read the New Testament from the beginning. I decided to learn a chapter by heart and then learnt one after another. I don't know why. I didn't know what I was looking for. I started reading the Bible to others at work, but I would start to read it and I would cry. I was so glad to have this Word I cried. It was such a precious treasure for me to have in my hand!

So Olga was born in 1992. They told me she might have Down's syndrome. They said that they would do further tests as it was not certain but I think they did not tell me clearly then because they did not want to make me too sad. I was a nurse so I knew all about Down's syndrome. I went out of the Doctor's room into the corridor and I knelt down there in the corridor. I did not care what people thought of me. I looked up and I cried out to God with a loud voice. I was sobbing. It was then I felt a power lifting me up as if I had wings. I wiped my eyes and I became quiet! I was still not converted then but I knew that God had helped me. I had addressed the only One whom I knew could help me.

We moved to Chișinău from Telenești in 1996. I used to take Olga to the Ștefan Cel Mare Park to have a walk. We were walking through the park one day in August 2000 and there were Christians there. They were singing and there was a man preaching with a Bible in his hand. He was preaching from John 3:16. I listened to them and I wondered who they were. I thought to myself that I would go to their church and one of the women invited me to their church. I wanted to go but I didn't and the next Sunday I went to the park again with Olga and there they were again! The following Sunday Olga and I went to the Isus Salvatorul Church to the old building.

I loved going there but I cried when I could not take the Lord's Supper. I thought, 'I must repent and get my soul right with God.' But I didn't. Then a brother came to preach who was not from our church. The Holy Spirit worked so powerfully in my heart that after the preaching I knelt in the front of the church and asked the Lord to forgive me. I took Olga with me to the front of the church. I prayed with all my heart, 'Forgive me Lord because I have lived a life without sense and a life that has been useless.' I knew that the Holy Spirit was filling me and giving me prayer. I fell down in the presence of this God. The church was on its feet. I did not know what was going on. I only knew that I needed to be forgiven. I went out of that church as if I had wings.

The following Wednesday I was coming home from work. I had a gold necklace on and a young man got hold of me from behind holding my necklace and he broke the necklace and ran away with it. I was still alive and I prayed out loud for the Lord to bless him. I realised that the devil was tempting me.

I was baptised on March 4th 2001. The Tuesday before the baptism a car hit me as I was crossing the road. I woke up with the ambulance next to me. I refused to go to the hospital. I still went ahead with the baptism. I had bruises all over me. Praise the Lord there were 81 baptised that day with me!

After I was converted I had opportunities to speak to so many about the Lord! I was on fire and very sad if people didn't want to listen to me speaking about Him. When others accepted God's Word it was such an encouragement to me. I spoke to them all about Jesus. I often spoke to Orthodox priests too and a nun.

God is everything to me now. When I open my eyes each morning I praise His sovereignty and His great power in creation, His holiness and His perfect Being. I start praying like that. It is as though my heart is filled with fire. I don't look at the things around me. We have a tiny apartment (four people live in one room and when it rains the water streams down the walls and when it is winter it is very cold), but the Lord never leaves us without. My greatest longing is that my son and husband will repent and follow the Lord. How can the world stand careless in the face of such a great salvation? What would I do without this

God? We will meet with death—I don't worry about any of it—God holds my hands tightly and I trust Him with everything. My heart and my life are full of praise to Him.

Olga and I often pray for others. The Lord says where two or three are gathered there I am. We kneel down and pray in the little space we have. 8 p.m. is the hour of prayer but not only then. We give such a high priority to prayer. And the Lord has worked. Prayer has great power. I love praying.

When I received chemotherapy I used to kneel on the grass outside the hospital and entrust myself into His arms. I would say to the Lord then, 'I know that Your will is good and perfect.' I knew that my hair was going to fall out. I always thank the Lord because it is only by His mercy and longsuffering that we are spared. I don't expect the Lord always to reply immediately but when He does your faith grows and it spurs you on to pray further. He teaches us patience when He does not reply immediately. I am happy for Him to break all my plans but that His will is done! I pray believing with faith. I know He hears me. He is the God of my salvation.

I find it thrilling to hear from these dear saints how the Lord worked so powerfully in their lives. The context in which the revival took place was one of severe economic hardship and mass emigration. The Christians experienced these phenomena as much as anybody else as you will read in the next chapters.

12

ECONOMIC COLLAPSE

The social context in which the awakening in Moldova took place in the 1990s was one of severe economic collapse in the country. The extent of that collapse exceeded all other former Soviet Republics following the break-up of the Soviet Union. This was partly attributable to the secession of Transnistria shortly after independence, but also because of the serious disruption of trade that occurred when the Soviet Union fell. Moldova had sent its rich agricultural produce to markets throughout the Soviet Union previously and had received subsidised energy imports in return. This arrangement collapsed spectacularly with independence and Moldova found itself cut off from its export markets. As Russian energy costs adjusted to world levels the country faced astronomical increases in import costs. There was hyperinflation in the early 1990s. By the late 1990s Moldova's economy had shrunk to two-fifths of its late Soviet size. Moldova did take steps to move towards a market economy but this has failed to bring significant improvements to the lives of most Moldovans. Although there has been relatively strong economic growth since 2000, Moldova still ranks as the poorest country in Europe. Malnourishment and disease have increased since independence and life expectancy has fallen. The GDP is equivalent to many third world countries. Many rely on the black economy or small holding plots of ground to survive.

The fall in living standards has led to a great exodus of Moldovans leaving the country in search of work. It is estimated that this is somewhere between one fifth and one quarter of the work force. In the 1990s very many emigrated permanently to the USA and now Western Europe and Russia are the target areas for most. It is estimated that 500,000 Moldovans are working in Russia.

Moldova is deeply divided along ethnic lines. There is a mix of ethnic Moldovans, Ukrainians, Russians, Gagauzi, Jews and Bulgarians. Russian speakers were most apprehensive about the Moldovan (a dialect of Romanian) language being made the official language of state in 1989 and serious conflicts broke out as a consequence.

All these elements provided a turbulent social backcloth to the revival. It is interesting to look at how the church dealt with these crises and reacted to these conflicts.

Firstly the economic crisis in the 1990s affected all those I spoke to and interestingly those memories were still very vivid to them.

Sister Aurica, whose husband had been a former KGB officer related the following story:

With the fall of the Soviet Union we experienced terrible poverty. Everything disappeared from the shops and Ghena [her husband] had no salary as he used to be paid from Moscow. We went through great difficulties. I was not working then. I can remember in 1994 during the winter I had used the last piece of bread and I had given Eugen, our son who was born in 1994, the last soup we had to eat which had been made with a cube. Ghena was expected home and there was no food, no bread and no money. I prayed on my knees for the Lord to send a scrap of bread to our house. I got up and there was someone at the door with a big loaf of bread—it was a friend who had brought it. This friend worked in a bread factory and they gave staff bread and she had thought of me. She brought some cakes as well. I am so thankful to her. I will never forget her—she was later converted and goes to church now. God answered my prayer! God hears our prayers!

Brother Petru recalled:

Most people were in despair because of the situation in the country. All their plans were broken in a moment and they had no hope, no work and no future as far as they could see. Money had become worthless and we were using coupons for a time instead of money. I can remember that my parents sold a bull and the sale only produced enough money to buy a raincoat.

Brother Serghei commented:

People may not have had bread to eat then but so many realised that Jesus is the Bread of Life. When man is left with nothing he has only God to turn to. When we are materially well off we don't see our need.

THE LATTER RAIN

Pastor Andrei, the elderly pastor who had been in Siberia, tried to help those in great need:

After 1990 the Soviet power was broken and chaos began. The 1990s were very difficult times for all of us. The factories stopped operating and there was very great despair everywhere but then God brought a great awakening. There was enormous suffering and hardship but the awakening started in about 1992 and went on for ten or twelve years. We are so thankful that many missions from Europe helped us then with material aid and with food and clothing. I can remember I was going through Cricova and I saw an elderly former teacher crying. She was in her 70s and she said she was ashamed to say that there was no food at home and no heating. I rushed to try to get something for her from members of our family and others and then I took what I could find to her and she cried for joy.

There was another woman I remember. She was alone with five young children and no food and no work. It was freezing in the house and they were all starving. I tried to get food and clothes for her too. Many came for help when they heard we had received humanitarian aid from the West but they also listened to the Word and many of those repented. It was a great wave of repentance—such a great movement of God that I never saw before then and have never seen since. It was the latter rain. People of all ages were drawn to repentance and faith: the old, the sick, children, adults, people from every kind of background. We prepared packages here in the church and took them round the houses every day. There was an old man we visited who had no fire and no food. I had rarely seen such poverty and there was nobody to help him. People couldn't afford to pay for burials so we arranged burials and we preached and sang at the services.

Another pastor shared a poignant story with me:

During the 1990s it was very poor indeed here. In 1997 a colleague from Romania came here unexpectedly with an American to supper. I gave them all that I had for supper which was bread and margarine and I broke some twigs from the sour cherry trees and boiled them up in water to make tea. They didn't say anything. It would not have been good if I had more than the church members. I needed to understand them and they had nothing. Some of them were starving. But the church was growing.

Brother Dumitru said:

The economic state of the country during the 1990s was terrible. It was as if everything had been destroyed which led to a general despair. People were looking for hope and they looked for God. So very many had no work and many had no food. People cried out for God.

GOD HELPED US THROUGH

Sister Natalia added:

Many were without work and those in work sometimes did not receive their salary for a year. We learnt to trust in God. He enabled us not to lack for our needs then. Somehow we got through it all. Sometimes we would receive grocery produce from over the border and by different means God helped us through.

Sister Tamara recalled:

I left work and soon after that my husband's hours were cut at work. Life was hard for us for quite a period. We used to look for things lying in the road—sometimes we found a coin and then we would buy a loaf. I wasn't converted then. But I realised that the Lord brought us through that difficult time.

Sister Lidia remembered:

Those were very difficult times. Many were not receiving their salaries and there were no pensions. My son's money was stolen by some young people at college with him. One day they took his watch too. But they asked him if he was a believer and the next day they gave him his watch back.

I first went to Moldova in 1998 and I can remember that the main city Chișinău resembled an industrial wasteland then with many of its main factories closed. There had been severe shortages of soap and shampoo and jokes were common about almost the entire population being nit-infested as a consequence. The electricity was cut off at very frequent intervals. Burglary and theft were commonplace as well as attacks on individuals carrying money or valuables and such attacks were often quite brazen. There was, I noticed, a great dependence on Western humanitarian aid amongst the Christians and indeed still is.

EMIGRATION

Moldova is a small country which has had to cope with mass emigration since 1990. Confronted with political instability, collapsing incomes and rapidly rising unemployment people began to emigrate on a large scale in the first half of the 1990s. It is estimated that up to 2 million Moldovans (from a population of 4.4million) are working abroad, very many illegally. Accurate statistical information is very hard to come by because of the fact that so many are working on the black market. Human trafficking is a prominent feature of this enormous outflow. There are serious political, economic and social consequences from this mass exodus but there are also very important and in some ways tragic implications for the church. In my experience it would still be the aspiration of most young people in Moldova to go to live and work in the West. Most extended families would have a member or several members working abroad. In the villages it is common to find a grandmother or older sibling looking after young children whose parents are working abroad. The numbers of those emigrating, which included very many Christians, had a marked effect on church growth during the revival, as the greatest exodus was taking place during the time of the revival. Pastors and choir leaders were the first to leave.

Brother Serghei sadly related some of the effects:

After 1995 mass migration to the USA began. There was a huge exodus and pastors and choir leaders were the first to leave. They had connections and they knew how to write a request for refugee status and they understood the system. They were able to locate sponsors even if these were only sponsors on paper. Ordinary members did not leave in such great numbers. Churches here suffered as a consequence of this mass exodus and the new leaders were from another generation who had not grown up in the work. Leadership in the churches as it were skipped a generation. There are hardly any old pastors here, the pastors are generally those who came into the work in the 1990s.

Brother Ghileţchi said:

Many believers emigrated during the 1990s. About 500 church members each year were emigrating and the total number would have been between 12,000 and 15,000 but these numbers do not include their family members and children who would not have been church members.

Brother Mihai's view was:

There was a great spiritual awakening, but so many emigrated from Moldova. About 30,000 Christians have left! This has had big repercussions in geo-political terms. If they had stayed Moldova would have been very different.

A GENERATION OF OLDER MINISTERS MISSING

Pastor Pavel commented:

> So very many have emigrated. From Bethel Church alone between 1990 and today we have lost 1000 members through emigration and another 1000 if we include the children that also left. So very many have left. So many new Christians were converted but a generation of older ministers was missing who would have helped them in their Christian walk and this was a great loss to the churches. In 1992 I got permission to emigrate to the States with my family but we decided to remain here. I was from a family with ten children and nine of my siblings are now living in the States. I stayed because I went to live in Germany for a year with my family but I didn't like the spiritual situation there. My children were adolescents at the time and I thought it would be better for them spiritually in Moldova. I have visited my family several times in the States and I'm convinced that we made the right decision to remain here.

Brother Vasile said:

> I had been a history student in the State University here and I was a convinced atheist. During my school years I had been secretary of the Komsomol. A professor in the university who was an atheist recommended that we read the Bible. I used my whole month's income to buy a Bible on the black market and I read it all the way through. I believed the God of whom it spoke and developed a deep love for Christ and yet I could not understand how anyone could live by those principles. I had become involved in criminality.
>
> On 27th November 1991 I was born again. During the next two weeks I read the whole Bible again. I longed to know the Scriptures better. But how could I do this? There was no-one to

teach me. I had no idea about churches but someone showed me a Baptist church in Chişinău and I was baptised. I met a group of Romanians living abroad who were developing Bible study materials. Their influence marked my whole Christian life. They are still my mentors today. Today there is a generation of orphan pastors in Moldova.

Brother Dumitru:

During the revival, emigration to the States began. I think this phenomenon had a negative influence on mission in the churches. Some who had a great zeal for God emigrated. In our church many of those who had been very active in the early 1990s emigrated and very many pastors emigrated. They included the pastor who had baptised and counselled me and encouraged me to preach and sent me for theological training. The tide of emigration disguised to some extent the real growth in the churches.

Most of the pastors I interviewed were in their 40s. There were a very small number of older pastors interviewed but I realised that many of that generation had left. What impressed me powerfully was that those who had elected not to emigrate did so with a strong sense that God had called them to remain and serve in Moldova. Almost all of those younger pastors who are now in their 40s and 50s could have left—they would have had the opportunity but they had decided not to go. And the Lord has mightily honoured their sacrifice in staying behind. I have watched their lives being spent out for God in a context which remains tough and I have seen their commitment to stay and to do that with contentment and joy.

The effects of the economic collapse in the 1990s together with the mass emigration which has affected most extended families in some way or other are still keenly felt by all those with whom I spoke and indeed all those whom I know. So the awakening began at a time when there had been a dearth of the Scriptures in the land and when opportunities for preachers and pastors to have theological training had been non-existent.

The following chapter traces something of the early attempts to introduce theological training to Moldova.

13

THEOLOGICAL TRAINING

*W*hile Moldova had been under the subjection of the Soviet Union, it remained cut off from outside theological influences and also devoid of theological literature as well as theological training for its ministers.

A former Baptist Bishop of Moldova told me:

Under Gorbachev there was more liberty for the first time. The trouble was that we weren't prepared for this new liberty as churches. We had lived for years under Soviet Communism and we had not been allowed any kind of theological education or access to higher education. There were slightly more opportunities for training in Romania. For instance, Bucharest had a theological college even if few students were allowed to attend it. Groups of preachers met secretly in other places to undertake some theological training in the 'School of the Prophets' in Romania. There was slightly more freedom in Romania marginally speaking. Here usually there was not the slightest chance that a Baptist could get into higher education and there were no opportunities for theological education at all. We were not prepared. The church was growing fast and we did not have men trained to preach.

In 1990 in the whole of Moldova there were two full time pastors each of whom had churches with over 1000 members. The church in Bălţi had about 1700 members and the church in Chişinău about 1500. There were 126 churches in the rest of the country. A few had congregations of 200 or 400. Atheistic propaganda stopped in 1990 and there was a famine for the Word of God and a great spiritual hunger in Moldova but we were not ready for this. But the Lord was so good to us. He loved us greatly and He took us into a time of great blessing.

THE MISSION SCHOOL BEGINS

We wanted to open a theological college to train the brothers. There were new churches everywhere and we didn't have trained preachers. There was a theological school in Moscow with teaching material and in the beginning we used their material. We started a Mission School in Bethel Church and began to teach. The course lasted for one or two years and the students would come for a week once every three months. There were about 32 or so students attending each course. We taught in Romanian translating from the Russian material we obtained from Moscow. Brothers came to help us from Great Britain and America. They knew we were in great need. We told them what we needed. Our need was so urgent and it was immediate. [Some problems did develop because some of the teachers who came from abroad were liberal both in their theology and in their lifestyle]. We had been completely cut off in the Soviet Union.

[It is worth noting here that as a result of this isolation liberal theology had never affected Moldova. When I first spoke to friends about liberal theology they had no idea what I was talking about. It was only gradually that I realised that the strict border controls in the Soviet Union had effectively kept liberal theological books and influence out of the country].

THE BIBLE INSTITUTE IN ORADEA

After the Revolution, a Bible Institute had started in Oradea, Romania and the brothers in Moldova proposed that we send some students there. Brother Iosif Ţon came here and the students did an entrance exam here. Some of our brothers including Brother Ghileţchi went to Oradea to study and others went to Bucharest. Ion Miron went to Bucharest. We had to fight to get visas and passports for them all. We rented a bus and took them to Oradea.

I became bishop in 1994. I was young and wanted to study as well but Brother Ţon said to me, 'You need to choose either to go, or to send these young men and stay on the front line preparing others.' Those brothers who were sent came back and are serving faithfully in our churches now. Brother Ghileţchi was instrumental in starting the Bible Seminary here—a building was bought on the site of the former Hebrew synagogue.

I realised a little of the sacrifice the dear brother who was speaking to me had made in giving up the thought of theological training himself to enable others to go to Oradea.

Brother Petru was one of the first students in the mission school organised to train preachers which took place in the Bethel Church:

I came back from the army in 1991. My parents were encouraging me to preach but I was shy by nature. In 1992 a mission school was organised in Chişinău and I attended. There were 32 of us. It helped me a lot. I learnt how to lead a church, how to expound

God's Word and how to search the Scriptures. It was a very good course and I learnt so much. I was the only ordinary church member on the course—the others were pastors or deacons already. In the village where I came from we had no in-depth Bible teaching.

The course finished and I went back to my village for two years to help in the work there and then I was asked to help in Harul (Grace) Church in Chișinău.

It was fascinating to listen to Brother Nikolai's account:

When liberty came we did not expect it and we did not know what to do with it. At the time of my repentance the aisles of our church were full with those on their knees repenting of their sins. There were three baptisms that year alone [1990] with about 200 people converted in our church that same year. Pastors became tired just with baptising such large numbers. I remember we hardly talked about secular things. Almost all our conversation was about the Lord. And then when we left our friends' company we talked to others about the Lord all the way home. We all did that. The Lord sent us a wind from heaven in the 1990s. The Holy Spirit worked so powerfully. We didn't use all the time as well as we should—we could have done more.

We did not have leaders well prepared theologically. The Mission School started in Bethel in 1992. We were not prepared for this great wave of people being converted and we had hardly any literature. We had only just got the Bible generally available. There was so much we did not know and much teaching had been from word of mouth. There is not enough good literature even now. We lacked literature and leaders and we were not prepared to counter the heresies that would come in.

SO MANY CHRISTIAN BOOKS!

Amongst the early students to be sent to train for the pastorate in Oradea, Romania was Brother Serghei from the church in Tiraspol:

> When I got to Oradea in 1995 and I went to the library and I saw how many Christian books there, I was absolutely amazed! I had no idea that so many Christian books even existed! I held a Bible atlas in my hand for the first time—you have no idea what a treasure that was for me! I was struck by the quality of the teachers there at the Bible Institute in Oradea. It was their character that impressed me and stayed with me even if I forgot some of the things they taught over the years. They were so full of love. And I never heard such preaching as I heard there! There was such great preaching and the messages had structure and were well prepared. The preaching of Brother Iosif Ţon really impressed me. I was impressed too by the hospitality of Christians in Oradea and I learnt that they had prayed for us. They received us as brothers. Often they were just simple people but they reached out to us and that really impressed me.

THE BEGINNINGS OF THE THEOLOGICAL COLLEGE IN MOLDOVA

Brother Ghileţchi trained in Oradea and then returned to Moldova and was one of those who helped to start the theological college in Chişinău. I will relate his story more fully as he was one of the key individuals in the movement towards setting up theological training in Moldova.

> I was born into a Christian family in the Soviet Union at a time when there was no freedom for the Gospel. After leaving school I went to a Technical College in Bălţi. Not long afterwards they

found out that I was a Christian and they told me that either I should join the Komsomol or I would be expelled from the college. A brother from Romania who was in our village spoke to me and advised me not to cede to this pressure and not to give in. I went back to the college and said to the Director if they expel me, so be it, but I could not agree to either of the options they presented me with but I did want to stay in the college. I remained in the college. Following that I was drafted into the Soviet Army and on my return I wanted to go the University in Odessa to study engineering. Brothers from the church in Bălți where I was a member said there was no point starting in university as I stood no hope of graduating as I did not belong to the Komsomol. I decided to go against the mainstream and said that by faith I will press on. No-one knew then in 1982 that perestroika would begin in 1985. I graduated from the university in 1988 and by then not only was Communism no longer obligatory as a creed but no one wanted to be a Communist. God had honoured my step of faith.

I became an engineer and then a chief engineer. In 1990 the opportunity opened up for me to go to Oradea in Romania to study theology. It was my dream to study theology. Brother Iosif Ţon came here in 1990 and recruited us to go to Oradea. I was one of the first students there. Others thought it strange that I went having already become a chief engineer. I knew Romanian already and I went to Oradea with my family. My wife learnt Romanian there.

During my second year in Oradea, Brother Victor Popovici who was the Secretary of the Moldovan Evangelical Baptist Union at the time, brought a TV crew to Oradea from Moldova to make a film about us students studying there. They did some filming and then they met us and I was interviewed. The journalist asked me what I was going to do after I graduated. His question really made me think but I replied immediately that I wanted to open a similar college of theology in Chișinău in

Moldova. Having articulated this and with time and talking to Brother Iosif Ţon it became clearer to me and in fact became the subject of my degree thesis.

I graduated and I came back to Moldova. Four or five of us worked together to set up what was then called 'Institul Sfânta Treime' [the Holy Trinity Institute] and it opened in 1994. Previous to this in 1992 a Mission School had been set up in Bethel Church by Feodor Mocan. In 1995 we joined the two schools together after discussion with the Baptist Union. We all agreed that it would be better to have one theological school, not two, and we became the Harul (Grace) College. I was Dean of the school and Feodor Mocan was the Director. We were together until 1998.

'THE LOVE OF GOD DREW US TOGETHER'

Some men called to the ministry went to Russia to study theology. Brother Alexandru was one such:

I got married in Bethel Church in 1991. A Mission School was formed in Bethel Church in 1992 called Mission Macedonia and some American teachers helped there. I was one of the students in the second entry from 1993 to 1994. I had an enormous thirst for the Bible and a burning desire to serve the Lord Jesus Christ. Previously the only opportunities were in the church services and Bible study groups under the oversight of the pastor. While I was in that first year Feodor Mocan came back from studying in St Petersburg. I had not realised that I might be able to continue theological studies further. I wanted to serve God better and have as much theological knowledge as I could. I went to St Petersburg for an interview and they offered me and a friend (who is now also a pastor in Betania Church) places in Year 2 of the Christian University. There was one condition: that we studied New Testament Greek intensively during the summer and attained good marks. I gained the very best marks possible. My wife and daughter came with me to St Petersburg and I studied there for a further two years and graduated with a Bachelor's degree in theology with the highest marks. I worked my way through those years to pay for the studies.

By 1996 there were already more churches in Chişinău and the College of Theology and Education had already been formed. Graduates from Romania and Russia combined to form the college. They were given the wisdom not to form two separate language colleges—the Lord led in this. The Lord so guided the brothers then that they kept unity and did not divide on the basis of language. The same is true of the Baptist Union—both language groups [i.e. Romanian and Russian] are represented in the same Union. At the fall of the Soviet Union we used the language to our advantage with an accent on mission. The language issue was not to our disadvantage. Our approach to mission has been multi-cultural and we have received strangers from abroad with love. We did not divide as the society around us was dividing. The love of God drew us together. The Lord did this amongst us at a time when we could not see what the future would bring. We need to obey God at each step and we will see the miracles of God. We should not be naïve but in terms of our faith we must be child-like. We must have a complete trust in the Lord and His Word. And we must learn to be faithful in the smallest things. Don't expect Him to trust you with big things if you do not learn to be faithful in small things. Be faithful to Him at every single step.

THE SPIRIT OF FIRE

Brother Anatol spoke of the beginnings of another large church in Chişinău and the impact of the return of brothers trained in Oradea to the church of which he was a member and pastor. The brothers returned to the continuing awakening.

You cannot explain what happened in Isus Salvatorul [Jesus the Saviour] Church humanly speaking. At the start there were 25 of us, weak and unprepared. And then there was an explosion! We were baptising 200 a year! There was a passion and a simplicity in our faith. We threw ourselves into the arms of God. It was all led by the Spirit of God.

We were not even ordained until 1996 although as young people we had preached very often. During the great awakening the church was overflowing with people and at the end we would eat together and then we would go to the park for open air evangelism all afternoon. Every Sunday in this way five or six people would be converted. Taking the Gospel to the parks on Sunday afternoons was greatly blessed. We gave out tracts and Gospels.

Brother Ghilețchi returned from training in Oradea and then Brother Fedula went to Oradea to train. When Brother Fedula came back he had such an impact on the young people. Every Tuesday evening the church was full of young people and very many were converted. Every Sunday many people were being converted. The awakening in our church started amongst the young people. We started the nights of prayer then. Hundreds of young people were praying for their country. There was such a spirit of prayer!

We must be on fire with praise for God! We allowed the Spirit to work. That fire still burns in me. You can change the service as much as you want but it's the Spirit of fire we need. God has His people and His time to work. He orders the right man to be in the right place at the right time. It was all brought together then. It was not easy but we need to use the time when it is ripe to work. There is a time when God is working.

I was teaching in the Bible Institute in Oradea, Romania in the 1990s and I remember seeing some of the Moldovan men who had been sent to study theology there. They struck me as serious and dedicated men. A number of them had to attend a preliminary Romanian language learning year as they were Russian speakers. They struggled financially during those years of training. In those early days the Bible Institute had no settled building and teaching would take place in rooms wherever they could be found. A number of the Romanian students there had been converted in the revival which took place in Oradea and that part of Romania in the 1970s. Many often spoke in those days of that revival of which they had been eye-witnesses. All of us benefited greatly from the preaching of Brother Iosif Ţon and Brother Paul Negruţ during those years. There may not have been much in the sense of good teaching conditions or resources but my memories of those years are of the great blessing I received through the students and of a vibrant spiritual context.

I turn now to consider some of the fruit of the revival and I will begin by looking at the developing missionary vision that was given to the brothers who led the theological college.

III

PART THREE: REVIVAL—
FRUIT IN ABUNDANCE

14

THE FRUIT OF REVIVAL

A MISSIONARY VISION

*W*e have seen how the College of Theology and Education was set up in the 1990's in Chișinău. This College latterly became a Christian University. I taught social work there for many years and managed to interview one of the founder members and leaders of that establishment. I will give his story in full as he was such a key person in the development of this work. His name is Brother Mihai.

In my childhood I dreamt of studying theology and becoming an international teacher of the Gospel. When I married my wife in 1985 she knew of this and she told me she was ready for whatever this could mean. I told my wife that I believed the Lord would open a door for me to go abroad to study theology. Five years passed and nothing happened. Three children were born to us and it looked as though my dream was impossible but I still had this dream. I told my wife that I thought God would take me to a capitalist country. My wife joked with me that I was a dreamer but my dream lived on.

A VISIT TO SOUTH KOREA

In 1989 I was one of the six leaders of the young people's work in Moldova. An International Congress of the Baptist Union was to be held in South Korea and I met with the brothers here to be considered as one of those to go to the Congress. Eleven people went from Moldova. I was put on the reserve list but I did go. They were nearly all older brothers besides me, but I was able to go despite the fact that they told me that Moscow might refuse my application.

We visited very large churches there and attended a baptism of 10,000 people. The Congress lasted for ten days but we were able also to visit churches in South Korea. Everything impressed me. It was the first time that delegates from the Soviet Union were able to attend the International Congress.

TO ROMANIA

It was at the Congress that I met the delegation from Romania— there were twelve of them. I learnt that five men from Moldova would be able to attend the theological seminary in Bucharest. I met Dr Vasile Taloş and he invited me to study at the seminary. My family remained at home. I did not have a grant but they provided me with somewhere to stay and food and they provided the lectures free of cost. My wife supported me wholeheartedly in all this and her parents were also a great support to us and the family. In all I studied there for four years. I used to return home to the family each month and then for three months in the summer. My brothers and I had formed a co-operative so that meant I had some financial reserves with which to support my family while I studied.

In 1992 the rouble lost value overnight and we lost everything. That meant that we no longer had any money in reserve to see us through crises. My wife and children moved to be with me in Bucharest after two years and my wife cared for a person who was blind to help support us.

STARTING THE THEOLOGICAL COLLEGE

In 1994 we returned to Moldova and four of us started the theological college here—that is Brother Namesnic, Brother Ghilețchi, Brother Miron and myself. In 1998 we started a school of social work, Veronica Pozdirca having returned from Oradea. [Veronica was one of my social work students in Oradea and she was the person through whom I first came to Moldova—it was at her request initially. Veronica is now living in the States]. Also in 1998 Brother Victor originally from Găgăuzia, returned from studying theology in Oradea. He suggested that we start preparing missionaries for Turkey. [Gagauz is a Turkic language]. We did have students from Găgăuzia (an autonomous Republic within Moldova) but many of them had not completed ten classes and their academic level was not very high as they were not always keen to study.

LOOKING EASTWARDS

It became apparent to us in 1998 that five or six of the ex-Soviet Republics—Kirghizstan, Azerbaijan, Tadjikistan, Kazakhstan and Uzbekistan—spoke Turkic dialects and they also spoke Russian. That realization helped us to take another step, to recruit students from those countries, from former Muslim backgrounds to train them here in Moldova. We were clear about our desire to do this but at the time we did not have the necessary means for such an undertaking.

In the same year, 1998, a group came from the USA and said they would sponsor as many students as we could bring from Central Asia. Some of them also helped us with the building of the Theological College.

In 2000 the chance arose for me to study for a doctorate in the State University in Bucharest. Having been accepted to study, I was thinking about using the opportunity to do something about the Islamic world. The night before I was due to present my proposal to the Commission for Doctorates I was in real turmoil because I did not know what to do. I was praying, but had no clarity about what to present to the Commission. It was at that point that God spoke to me about what to do. I know His voice and I recognised it. It was a very powerful experience. I knew I had to write about the Islamic world and an outline came to me. The next day I went to the Commission and presented my ideas which were about a contemporary paradigm of the Gospel for Christian mission to Muslims in ex-Soviet Republics of Central Asia.

Students from Central Asia started to come here and I visited Central Asia for the first time in 2000. That was how I got my material for the doctorate. I forged links with the underground churches and I met groups secretly and started working with them. Students were sent here through these contacts.

Having discovered many unregistered churches in those countries we realized that we also needed to prepare workers there in their own country.

Visits were made two or three times a year to Central Asian Republics by teachers from our school to train students. I used to go frequently and the border authorities would ask me why I was visiting. I could tell them that I was studying for a doctorate on the Islamic world. It was a very good means of entry to me for about seven years or so and in this way I obtained my material. 400 students from Central Asia have graduated from our school. In 2004 we also opened a social work course for them. [There had previously been a social work course for Romanian speaking students only].

My studies revealed that until the 14th Century there was a Nestorian Christian community in each of these countries, which subsequently disappeared. With the fall of the Soviet Union there was another wave of God's grace for these lands. Although German and Russian Christians had lived in these places they had not generally taken the Gospel to the Islamic world in which they found themselves. In 2000 there were about 5000 to 10,000 Christians in each of these countries. We wanted to prepare Christian workers from amongst them. It was a common experience that after conversion to the Christian faith such believers would be rejected by their family and by society and they would not have any means of livelihood. We concluded that we needed to develop a whole system of training for them which included theology, social work and business skills. Converts from Islam very often lose their jobs as well as their relatives and they need a means to support themselves.

TO THE UTTERMOST PARTS OF THE EARTH

We need to be able to read the times we are living in and a new vision is developing. A multitude of Muslims are now working in Russia. Moscow alone has millions of Central Asians living there —conservative estimates say the figure is 4 million. I was teaching in Moscow last year and just through my own observations I could see that there were about three times as many Central Asians than Russians on the streets and in the shops. It is said that Moscow is no longer a Russian city.

By 2014 in Siberia, main centres of population such as

Ekaterinberg, Omsk and Tobolsk each had Muslim populations of between 200,000 and 400,000. The choice is either that they are evangelised or they will Islamise any country in which they find themselves. Our vision now is to open a school for Muslims of the diaspora in Siberia. It is easier to reach them when they are not in their own country. They are more vulnerable and everyone wants to profit from them. Our vision is about providing them with work and somewhere to live and a small income and at the same time using the opportunity to teach them the Gospel.

Brother Alexandru, a pastor who also teaches theology in the same school said:

> We never thought that the Lord would use us to change the world and particularly the Muslim world. The Gospel has changed us and we are always seeking to do more and more in mission. Moldova sends missionaries over the border.

So once again this tiny country was used and is being used powerfully of God to reach out with the Gospel eastwards. Having taught for a number of years with these brothers I have been staggered by the extent of their vision. I remember that years ago, one of them said to me, 'The time is *now* whilst so many throughout Central Asia still speak Russian. By the next generation it will be too late. We must act now.'

This extraordinary missionary vision was one of the fruits of the awakening. Another fruit of the revival and the newly found border freedoms was the distribution of the Scriptures throughout the country. The Gideons (an international organisation whose work is to distribute the Scriptures) played a key role in this as the next chapter will describe. The translation and extensive use of inductive Bible study materials throughout the country was another means of building up the new converts and that story follows in the next chapter.

15

'GOD CHOSE THE SMALLEST COUNTRY TO DO GREAT THINGS'

One very important goal in the wake of the new freedoms and the revival was to get the Scriptures distributed as widely as possible throughout Moldova. Few had a copy of the Bible at the end of the 1980s. The unregistered churches had been the most successful in the secret printing and distribution of the Scriptures but those in the registered churches were much less well supplied.

THE WORK OF THE GIDEONS

Brother Pavel, who continues to this day to lead the Gideon work, shared:

The Gideons' work started in Moldova in 1989. This was the first Gideons' work in the whole of the former Soviet Union. God chose the smallest country to do great things! It happened like this: after a Thursday evening church service the pastor (who is in the States now) read out a list of 25 people to stay behind. We did not know why we were being asked to remain behind. Then someone came to speak to us who was the head of the Gideons in

Europe. He talked about their work and said that they wanted us to set up a work here and distribute the Scriptures in schools, prisons and hospitals. We looked amazed at him as we did not have any Scriptures for ourselves then let alone for distribution to others! He told us that they would give us as many copies of the Scriptures as we needed. We couldn't believe our ears!

SUCH GREAT JOY!

We prayed every Monday for two years for the Lord to send us Scriptures to distribute. Then a brother from Germany brought us 2,000 copies of the New Testament in Russian. We took them around the schools and they produced such great blessing and joy —we were surrounded by those asking for the Scriptures! Then a truck with 120,000 New Testaments came! We went through all the schools in the country giving out something like 10,000 New Testaments in a week. Everywhere they were received with such great joy.

We were amazed at how the Lord changed everything here. We have given out over 4 million copies of the Scriptures in Moldova. And now we are giving out between three and four thousand New Testaments a year. During the 1990s when we were giving out the Scriptures in schools we were often asked to take religious lessons for an hour or so afterwards.

Once when I was in a church in Singerei Noi and I was in the vestry before the service, one of the brothers said he knew me. I said I didn't know him. He said, 'I was in the Republican Hospital and you gave me a New Testament about ten years ago. I read it and now I'm a preacher in the church.' I could tell you of hundreds of cases like that. In our group of Gideon helpers there are those who were converted through reading our New Testaments. The Word has great power. Sometimes we don't even have to speak. There was such a time when so many had a great hunger for God. As it says in the Scriptures, if God opens a door no man can shut it.

STUDYING THE WORD

Parallel with the distribution of the Scriptures throughout the country the translation and widespread use of inductive Bible study materials did much to strengthen the new converts. Detailed Bible study notes were prepared and leaders trained to open up the Scriptures in small groups. Brother Vasile Filat was one of the men instrumental in this movement. He shared with me also his perspective on the revival:

> I can remember that during the 1990s I went back to my home village on a visit. I was talking to some of our neighbours and in no time at all, about a hundred were listening to me preaching the Gospel. This is an example for you to understand the times then. But I think we only used a tiny fraction of the opportunity we were given then. There was so much potential to have won the whole country for Christ but leadership was missing. It all happened so spontaneously. There was such an openness to spiritual things and such an interest in the Gospel and all the freedoms we could have wished for! It was such an opportunity.
>
> By contrast in 1920 the church had very good leaders with great vision in a context that was hostile and harsh but there was great fruit from their ministry. In 1920 there were only six Baptist churches in Moldova but by 1940 there were 18,000 believers not including their families. During the 1990s there was a great wave of revival. It is true that many emigrated but many of them were able to plant some of the biggest Protestant churches in Western Europe, for example in Rome. They became an instrument of the awakening where they were. And they were able to help the work here financially.
>
> Inductive Bible study has been very important in the

preparation of workers. There has been a great vision for this work throughout Eurasia. Those attending undertake two weeks intensive Bible study and they are equipped to teach others. That work started in 1997 here in Moldova. It has played an enormous role in preparing leaders and in church planting. There are beautiful results from this work.

I WANTED TO BE AN ORTHODOX PRIEST

Brother Andrei was influenced by these Bible study materials and came into contact with Brother Vasile through this means. A Gideon New Testament had been instrumental in his coming to Christ.

I was born into an Orthodox family in Olăneşti. The Orthodox church in our village had been destroyed but every Easter I used to go with my grandmother to the neighbouring village where there was an Orthodox church.

In 1990 when the borders opened I was 14 years old and I decided that I wanted to train to be a priest and to train in Kiev. There was no Orthodox seminary here then, you had to go to Kiev or Odessa to train.

People had started going to church in those days. There was a very quick change in allegiance superficially. Communists became religious overnight and became friendly with the priests. It was possible for the first time to speak openly about God. Priests started to gain a high status in society. But I realised that my family wanted me in the priesthood from financial motives: the mayor was planning to build a house for the priest and his family and an Orthodox church. This was a great disappointment to me and I decided not to train. I wandered away from the Orthodox church.

I came to Chişinău and during my first year in University I got involved with a bad crowd. We were involved in illegal money exchange and we cheated a lot of people. I began using alcohol so much that I had no memory of what I had done the previous evening. I would also smoke my way through three packets of cigarettes a day. I became a very heavy drinker and got through enormous quantities of alcohol. Everyone was afraid of our group. About that time I got into trouble with the police.

WHAT IS THE PURPOSE OF YOUR LIFE?

Then my friend Boris kept asking me to go to hear Victor Gam preach. It was 1993 and there was a big evangelistic outreach in Chişinău. One evening I was drunk and I agreed to go just to shut him up. He had been inviting me for a whole week. Victor Gam asked the same questions that had been on my mind: 'Why are you alive? What is the purpose of your life?' I was 18 and I knew that my only purpose was drink, enjoyment, cigarettes and learning. I listened carefully to the message and when I got back to the hostel I looked for a Gideon's New Testament that I had been given at school but which I had never opened.

I used to go back to my home in Olăneşti every Friday and I took the New Testament which I was reading with me. I read the whole New Testament to try to find answers to the questions which had been troubling me. Then I went to the priests in the Orthodox church but they couldn't answer my questions. I realised then clearly that they gave more importance to their books and traditions than the Bible and I understood that I had to stick with the Bible.

Boris took me to the Isus Salvatorul Church [Jesus the Saviour Church]. They were meeting then in the old building but the foundations for the new church were being laid and I used to help with the building work. At that time I was seeking the Lord. Then I went to a screened transmission of Billy Graham preaching which was at the Palatul Naţional (the biggest concert hall in the city). I realised so clearly then that I could not conquer my sin in my own strength. I wanted to change and for three months I tried to change myself in my own strength but I couldn't do it. Then I saw that only God could help me. That day I prayed to the Lord and said, 'Lord I have no power. Only you can change me, please change me!' From that day on I no longer lived in habitual sin. I hated even the smell of cigarettes from then. God gave me the power to overcome sin and I was converted.

I realised that I needed to study the Bible and I started doing inductive Bible studies with Brother Vasile. At that time we visited all the churches throughout Moldova teaching methods of Bible study. I found that my questions were always being answered from the Bible and I saw how crucial personal Bible study was for me and as a means of showing others the Way.

After I was converted my parents rejected me and said I was no longer their child. They wouldn't financially help me any longer. My grandparents said that God does not exist; these were the same grandparents who had wanted me to be an Orthodox priest. They said it was all too much, too much faith, too much Bible. When they discovered that I was going to be baptised they turned their backs on me too.

THE LORD TOOK CARE OF ME

I had no work nor food nor heating and it was winter. But every evening I went to a prayer meeting or took part in evangelism or I went to a Bible study. I never asked God why I didn't have those things. I didn't know what I would eat the next day but the Lord took care of me. It made me trust Him so much more! It made me grow in faith and I looked to Him. I believed all His promises. I studied His Word and I believed it.

I remember that during the 1990s during evangelistic meetings the tents and the meeting places would be so full there was not enough room. There was never enough room for everybody. In the Palatul Naţional there were so many people listening to the Gospel that you could hardly breathe. There was never enough room in the churches either and you often had to stand outside to listen, or you would be inside the church and perspiring because it was so full and so hot. There were services every day. So many people were looking for God! When I used to travel on the trolleybus I always took some Bible study material with me and I would use every journey to talk to someone about the Gospel. The Communists used to tell us there was no God. They used to promise everything but in the end people were so disillusioned. They wanted to know about eternity and they began to seek for God.

I have often attended the Bible study groups referred to and have used the published materials this movement have made available to my great spiritual profit. Such was the anointing on the men who led those Bible study groups that I can remember their teaching years on from the events in question and have marked memories of the way in which the Lord Himself met with us as the Word was opened up to us. We feasted on the Word of God and longed to study its teaching. Looking back I think they were all marks of that revival.

Another means greatly used of God to spread the Gospel and to build up the saints was the Christian radio ministry which was set up during the awakening and continues to the present day.

16

THE BEGINNINGS OF CHRISTIAN
RADIO IN MOLDOVA

*M*y interview with Brother Anatol took place in the Christian radio recording studio in Chişinău on a very hot day in September. I knew of him as a pastor and a preacher but had little previous understanding of his involvement in the radio ministry. So many people listen to Christian radio in Moldova and it is broadcast for 24 hours each day to every part of the country. Often I have visited homes where its programmes can be heard in the background and very large numbers of Moldovans from all kinds of backgrounds listen to it, including myself. I will share something of the background to Brother Anatol's eventual link to the radio ministry.

I was born into a Christian family. My grandparents were the first family to be converted in Bucovina and then my parents were converted. My parents presented Christ to us in a way that children would understand. My mother read a lot about heroes of the faith such as David and Daniel and I wanted to be like them. She had a delightful way of explaining those things to us and went over those accounts again and again. The love for God and for the people of God came from my parents.

During the 1970s I did not belong to the Komsomol or the Communist Party so there was no chance of my getting into higher education. I tried but did not succeed. I went into the army but there too we were looked down on. When I left it was difficult to find a job, but I worked in construction and also as a crane driver.

OUR DAUGHTER COULD NOT BREATHE

I was converted in Cernăuți [Cernăuți is in the Ukraine] and baptised in 1981 and then I started to study the Bible in earnest. In 1983 I married Mila. Our second daughter developed respiratory difficulties a year after the Chernobyl disaster. We were near the site of the explosion when my wife was pregnant and the baby was born with narrowed respiratory organs and she was placed in an incubator. Those problems lasted for a year or more and she was unable to breathe properly and her condition was getting worse. We thought that we might lose her. Lots of children in our area became ill after Chernobyl.

A doctor told us that we had to get out of Cernăuți if we wanted to save her life. We did not want to leave. I was working and we had a house there. But we sold up everything and came to Chișinău as my brother was there. So our daughter Ala brought us here in 1989. We became members in Bethel Church and I started to preach there. I started preaching the Gospel in villages too in about 1989.

At the end of 1990 I met Brother Florin and his wife Liliana for the first time in Bethel Church. [Brother Florin is a Romanian who has emigrated to the States. He visits Romania and Moldova very regularly and is committed to Christian radio ministry in both countries]. I can remember that he preached on Jonah and I was moved by his message. He came back to our house as he was Romanian and he told us about the way that 'Micul Samaritean'

[Little Samaritan—the name of the Christian radio station in Romania and subsequently in Moldova] had started in Romania and how he had started a work there with children and helped the poor. It was all new to me. I was already very involved in evangelism and at the new Isus Salvatorul Church but I accepted his request for help. We printed our first book, *The Good Samaritan for Little Children*, and that was the beginning of 'Micul Samaritean' in Moldova.

SUNDAY SCHOOL WORK BEGINS

We started to visit orphanages and in 1991 the mission 'Micul Samaritean' was registered. We tried to find material for Sunday School work. We prepared the material for Sunday School teachers using a flannelgraph for the lessons.

We trained teachers in Bălți in the north, in the centre and in the south of Moldova. At that time the notion of Sunday school was new, but the Baptist Union gave its blessing and in the end the work was blessed and grew.

The doors were open for the Gospel in orphanages and schools and 'Micul Samaritean' had a group of teachers who taught the Bible in schools. There were 25 teachers who taught the Bible daily in this way. We had about three or four years in the schools and then the doors started to close as Orthodoxy grew in power and influence. The Protestants got into action much more quickly than the Orthodox after the revolution. Even though access to schools weakened we still had access to the orphanages. We offered clothes and shoes on condition that we could preach the Gospel. There was a time when we were practically providing all the clothes and footwear for the orphanages. And we sowed the Word in those places. We left radios so that they could listen to Christian radio. These days we put radios in prisons too.

THE FIRST PROGRAMMES ON NATIONAL MEDIA

Brother Florin had recorded and transmitted children's programmes with Radio Free Europe and he asked me whether we could have them broadcast on the radio in Moldova. The first Christian programmes for children were broadcast on the national radio here in 1992. The TV also gave us time for children's programmes about then.

In 1992 I made my first visit to America. I went to visit a Christian radio station there that was situated in a little house with two small rooms and one person working there. I thought, 'Why don't we do that in Moldova?' I came back very keen to do something. We started to pray and to make enquiries about frequencies available and we talked to many people.

OUR OWN RADIO STATION

The Lord went before us all the time. The door to the Minister of Telecommunications opened. They gave us the first frequency for six hours a day. 'Micul Samaritean' was the first private radio station in Moldova. On July 11th 1994 the first programme was broadcast. We faced some big battles but they eventually gave us 24 hours broadcasting time a day. Sometimes we had better coverage than national radio. There were no specialists to help us then and it was a lot of broadcasting time to fill but God blessed it all. Brother Florin used to bring us suitcases full of cassettes with programmes.

A METHOD GOD CHOSE TO USE

There was such an impact from the radio! We had never

anticipated that churches would start as a result of the radio. From 1995 to 1997 we held nights of prayer and many used to pray for the radio. The church was full during those nights of prayer. The Lord used the radio to spread the Gospel throughout the country! It seemed that everyone was listening to the radio— in their homes, in hospitals! We only used to broadcast the name of the preacher and not the church he was from. Even priests were listening to the radio. My aunt said that her priest in Bucovina was preaching what he heard on the radio. It was a method God chose to use in the awakening. The Orthodox Church was very afraid of the influence of the Bible then but we wanted to reach everyone. The Bible is what transforms a person and 'Micul Samaritean' brought the Gospel to its listeners and encouraged them to read the Bible. The Minister of Telecommunications went home and said to his mother that the man on the radio had a more correct Bible than the priests. Many Orthodox believers listen.

The Lord gave Brother Florin a vision for radio and the Lord brought me to Moldova to serve. I would never have left Cernăuţi. My pastor there told me I was like Jonah when I left but I knew the Lord's peace in leaving and His assurance. And look how He has led me! My daughter Ala has not been in hospital for a day since we came here. She has been healthy and we see the hand of God in all this. There were others much better prepared than me here. I tried to get into the theological college in Oradea, Romania but Brother Iosif told me to go home and work. God prepared me in His school.

There is a great variety of programmes broadcast on Christian radio in Moldova—I speak as a listener here. Each day there will be powerful sermons by preachers in Romanian and Russian (programmes are bi-lingual). Not unusually I have been deeply convicted of sin as I have listened to the preaching on the radio— there was a work of the Spirit in the revival with regard to conviction of sin. There is often powerful teaching on the Cross of Christ and on the only way to find peace with God. Preachers often have a boldness in presenting the Word which compels the listener to heed the message. Some messages will be evangelistic and some will have rich and challenging teaching for the believer. There are daily programmes for children; testimonies and conversion accounts; musical programmes (Moldova has a great musical tradition and a rich repertoire of hymns and Christian songs) and much else. My own observations would confirm that it is avidly and very widely listened to throughout Moldova. What a wonderful means of bringing glory to Christ it has been!

Brother Anatol spoke of their mission's involvement in bringing the Gospel to orphanages. During and since the revival a multitude of efforts have been made by Christians in Moldova to reach those on the periphery of society who were suffering hardship. These have included orphans and children in institutions; prisoners; women who have been trafficked; adults and children with disabilities and elderly people to name just a few. The following chapter will begin to describe some of those efforts.

17

ORPHAN CHILDREN HEAR THE GOSPEL

J had been aware over the years of numerous efforts to bring the Gospel to children in Moldova, particularly children who lived in State institutions. My work as a social work lecturer in the Bible College had given me an inside perspective on some of this work. Without doubt there has been the most tremendous effort to reach such children with the good news of the Gospel both during and subsequent to the awakening. I would like to share some of those endeavours with you. I met Brother Leonid and his wife Sister Eugenia in a village in the north of Moldova where he related the following:

> My wife and I met in Bălți and my parents gave me their house in Sofia and we moved there. We arrived in Sofia in 1981 and I began preaching in the church there. In 1988 I was ordained pastor of the church.

WE COULD NOT GO WITH EMPTY HANDS

In 1991 we decided to try to reach orphan children with the

Gospel. In 1990 my wife gave birth to our fifth child and at the same time freedom for the Gospel came. We decided to start with orphanages near our village. There were 400 children in the orphanage in Drochia and 150 children in an orphanage near Drochia. But we felt that we could not go with empty hands so my mother and Sister Galia cooked and we took big bags full of bread they had cooked. We did not have transport and we were hitching lifts with these huge bags. But someone stopped for us and gave us a lift because they thought we were taking things to the orphanage. It was a miracle. They took us to the very courtyard of the orphanage and all the children surrounded us. It was damp and freezing cold and the children were filthy and their shoes were falling apart. The Director and the teachers came out to greet us and they were so glad we had come. The Director gathered all the children together in the hall. He said, 'Let's listen to what they would like to say to us.' I told them about the Lord Jesus. I asked them if they knew anything about Him. One lad said he had seen Him on a cross near the church. I told them that He is alive and I told them what He had done and I asked them if they wanted Him to be their friend. I believe that God gave me the message—the Holy Spirit was with us and after that our family started to pray for these children. That's how we started.

Soon we were visiting five orphanages regularly. Every day we preached and taught from the Bible and used the flannelgraph we had been given. If children had been taken to hospital we used to visit them there too. For two years there was hardly any electricity and we used to do all this using a torch. One day in an orphanage I noticed a huge crowd of children huddled near a single heater in the corridor. The whole heating system had frozen up because there was only two hours electricity every day. We came home exhausted and I thought to myself that we could not leave them like that. So we went round to our neighbours to borrow heaters. We found five small heaters and took them to the orphanage. Next day I went to the Department of Education in

Drochia and told them that they had to do something for those children. They moved them to a nice nursery in Drochia and we were allowed to go there as often and for as long as we wanted. The Director was so grateful to us for helping them.

After 1992 there was a change in the direction of the work. We decided to take some of the children into our own home. Every school holiday we would take about twenty children to live with our children. They learnt to play together. Sometimes they helped our neighbours. The neighbourhood was full of children! Then we took them after they finished school; at first there were twelve of them.

AUREL'S STORY

During the evenings around the table they would often talk to us about their past life. We were deeply moved by what they told us. One evening I asked a lad named Aurel to tell us something about his life. He was reluctant to speak.

I asked him what his surname was and he said, 'Otoman'. Immediately I remembered a newspaper headline I had read back in 1982 about a family with that name in which the father had killed the mother and the children had been left without parents to care for them and there were no relatives. I had written to the editor of the newspaper but he did not reply but I kept the article and I prayed for those children. It turned out that Aurel was one of the children! God had brought him to our house at the age of 14 after all those years! Aurel told us he did not know where his brother was. We found his brother Simeon in Fălești and we looked after the two brothers. Aurel was keen to be in our family but he was not interested in our faith and when we went to church he would stay at home and play the guitar and listen to Christian music cassettes.

One day Aurel came with us to church. It was a time in the

1990s when many young people were being saved in the awakening. He was converted and later he married my niece and they are living in America now with six children.

During the 1990s we went through a very difficult time. We had a house full of children and my husband had no job [pastors in Moldova almost always have to work in addition to their pastoral duties] and there was no means of supporting them. My parents advised us to send the children back. I used to sew day and night to buy the bare essentials for them. One day I had no idea how I would feed them the next morning. My ex-boss arrived at our house with two sacks of flour! I have never said to a child that they must go back to the orphanage.

We used to run a Christian library in the village and many young people and children used to borrow books from that library and then bring them back the next day. The Orthodox priest would tell them not to read the books but the Lord gave us wisdom in the work.

WE HAD TO LIVE THE GOSPEL

Another pastor described how their church grew in the 1990's and how they started to become involved in the needs of young people and children in institutions:

The years 1991 to 1996 presented an extraordinary opportunity for evangelism. We held services in all the surrounding villages and we planted churches in those villages firstly in 1996 in Chirca, then in 1997 in Todiresti, in 1998 in Ruseni and then in 2000 in Bulboaca. We were regularly holding baptisms of about twenty people at a time in our own church. So many were repenting. But then the exodus from the country started which affected all the churches.

During the 1990s I realised very clearly that it was not enough only to preach the Gospel—we had to live it and demonstrate its power in our lives. We started to work a lot in institutions all over the place. I have never heard the Lord's voice explicitly but I saw a need and I asked the Lord what I could do. There were so many children in the institutions. We rejoice in the resurrection of Jesus and how can we do nothing about them? A report on human trafficking said that 22% of the women who are trafficked are brought up in institutions. In 2001 two girls from institutions came to live with us. They have done well and they remained with us until they married. I felt the blessing of God on us through all this. When I read about human trafficking it made me feel very selfish and I realised that we needed to find families for these girls. By 2007 we had placed up to 200 children and young people in families. I have seen how the Lord can work! I worked for twenty-two years as an engineer and I would never have believed that I would become involved in this kind of work. So many of those we have worked with over the years have been converted.

(I should add that this same brother is involved in a huge work of outreach to elderly people, to adults in institutions and to orphans).

THE CHILDREN HAD THE SAME HUNGER FOR GOD

Christian camps work flourished at the same time. Brother Petru had a significant involvement in this ministry:

I was involved in camps work from about 1996 to 2003. About 400 children would attend each week in a camp designed for 320 children. The maximum number we catered for in one week was 420. The children had the same hunger for God as the adults and very many came to the Lord—hundreds and hundreds of children during those years. We held camps for five or six weeks each summer. It was a wonderful opportunity. When we were growing up there was no such thing as Christian camps and our parents would not allow us to go to the Communist Pioneer camps. We wanted to communicate to these children that although we need to be serious with God that there is great joy in the Christian life. It was a fruitful work.

Another pastor who was involved in a church plant in a suburb of Chişinău shared of their involvement with street children and with prisoners:

In 2001 we started to think about people outside the church who were suffering great distress. We developed seven social projects over the years and each of them appeared in a wonderful way. I went through the Gospel of Matthew with our church. We looked carefully at the Lord's call to us to go into all the world to make disciples verse by verse. All the time we were thinking of those who had not yet repented. We wanted so much to reach them and teach them. The vision is still very clear to us. We are involved in evangelism and social projects and the aim of each of these is to make disciples.

In 2001 the 'Hand and Heart' project started with children. It was a huge project. So many children came. There were many living underground and on the streets in those days.

PRISONERS BAPTISED

In 2004 the Nazareth project started with prisoners. I started a correspondence with a woman who had been in prison twice and she was converted. She wanted to be baptised after that and she was baptised in prison. At the prison in Rezina there were many 'lifers.' We met a prisoner who was chained to three others. He was to be shot but then the law changed and they did not know what to do with him. We brought the Gospel to him and he was saved. After a couple of months of working in the prison people were being saved and we were baptising them there. Even though lifers were not allowed to come to the services we used loudspeaker boxes so they could hear. We could not see them but we knew that many were listening to the messages. They used mirrors to see us. One man was baptised in chains and he took the Lord's Supper in chains too. They allowed us to have Bible studies and prayer with him that used to last for three hours. Then others started coming to those Bible studies and we were baptising even more of them.

After two or three years the prison gave us a room for worship. There was even a sign put up which said, 'Nazareth Baptist Church'. We called the project 'Nazareth' because one of the prisoners said to us, 'Can anything good come out of Nazareth?' We knew that with God the answer was yes.

A number of doctors and medical staff were converted during the revival and they determined to use their medical skills as a means of outreach to those who were not yet converted. Their story follows in the next chapter .

18

AN AWAKENING AMONGST THE INTELLIGENTSIA

*T*he revival led to the conversion of a large number of men and women who had achieved a high level of education and qualification in various professions during the Communist era. Amongst their number were many medically qualified staff who once converted, longed to meet the spiritual and health needs of their fellow Moldovans. Sister Eugenia is now one of the leaders of a Christian medical work which Brother Liviu heads up. She shared the following:

> During the awakening in the 1990's when Brother Liviu repented there was also an awakening amongst the country's intelligentsia. Many intellectuals were converted then and a new class of people appeared in our churches. We believe that the Lord's people need to be in all the social structures—in medicine, the government, in education and in every sphere of public life.

Brother Liviu about whom we have heard before in Chapter 7 and whose whole family was converted in 1990 started a medical work:

During the great awakening in our country many other doctors became Christians from all over Moldova. We came together in a united desire to serve the Lord. But first of all we wanted to strengthen ourselves in the Word. A Bible study for medical staff started.

The idea to have a Christian medical centre started in 1991. We prayed for six years and then in 1997 God replied. Churches throughout Moldova supported us in prayer and helped us to build this clinic. The church 'Isus Salvatorul' offered us the land on which to build and the medical centre was opened on 1st November 1998. Our aim was to spread the Gospel of Christ to patients and colleagues. We are full of joy that many other doctors and nurses heard the Gospel and some of them joined us in the work.

I needed to get a lot of official permissions to start the clinic and I had a lot of contact with Government officials and those from the Department of Health. Most of them received us warmly and supported us. There was such an openness to the Word then. In our church at the time there were three baptisms a year and 100 people were baptised at a time—that was 300 in a single year. There were so many evangelistic outreaches and people used to come in hundreds and thousands to hear the Word and so many received the Word with joy. We had free access to take the Gospel even into Government circles and into higher education. It was what God did and we rejoiced.

A BEAUTIFUL WORK

Sister Eugenia added:

I see how great the need is for people to know God and I am aware also of their material needs. God has put us in the place of His choosing here to be a light for Him. All our family are involved in serving Him and we are united in this desire. Each day we are involved in the medical work. We work hard but we love what we do. We hold mobile clinics and conferences and seminars each month. Each week there are meetings for medical students and we meet with doctors and medical teaching staff and share the Gospel. We organise meals for poor people where the Gospel is preached. Recently we organised a meal for carers who are looking after bed-ridden relatives at home. They enjoyed it so much and it provided a tiny respite for them. At Christmas we give out food parcels to all our patients. We offer free medical services in a number of places in the country. Many people come to us for all sorts of help. We distribute humanitarian aid in institutions and in prisons.

Last year we organised a meeting in a Casa de Cultură [community centre] near Aneni Noi. I was wondering who would come as it was cold and there was no heating and it was dark there. But the place was filled with people and we had to bring in more chairs as there were not enough for those who came. It lasted for three hours and when we spoke or sang you could see our breath it was so cold.

The Lord has given us a beautiful work to do. We don't know how long the Lord will give us liberty but we need to use every opportunity now while we have it. I rejoice in what we are doing.

The medical centre which forms the hub of this work is situated in an attractive, large building near the centre of Chişinău and on week-days will be full of patients and staff. Each day starts with a time of prayer and a short message for staff. On the occasions when I have been in this centre I have been struck by the kindness and concern of those who work there and of the way in which they communicate Christ's love to those with whom they work.

Very many churches in Moldova have a work amongst people who are poor and those who are sick, elderly people, children in need, women who have been trafficked and those with disabilities. There is a quite remarkable flourishing of such works up and down the land and I think this is a consequence of the revival.

REACHING ADULTS WITH DISABILITIES

Life for children or adults with disabilities in Moldova is not undergirded with the same kind of supports we would be familiar with in the West. There are still a number of very large institutions for adults with disabilities in the country. These formed the contact point for the beginning of our own work in Casa Mea so it was fascinating for me to interview men and women who worked in such institutions straight after the fall of the Soviet Union.

Brother Leonid and Sister Eugenia, of whom we heard about in Chapter 17 and their work with children in institutions, also worked in adult institutions. They worked in the same institution in the north as our own charity now works but they laid the pioneer work for the Gospel in that place. Those adults we know with disabilities who came into contact with them then in the 1990's still speak of them with enormous love and respect. Sister Eugenia spoke of their initial contact with this place.

A neighbour told us what a terrible state the institution was in. I said to my husband, 'Let's go there'. On our first visit I felt so awful because many of the people there were naked and they were shivering with the cold. I could not believe what conditions were like there. We were determined to keep visiting and we went every week to help those people and to take the Gospel to them. After a time the Christian radio, Micul Samaritean, bought a green car for us for the work and gave us coupons for the petrol. [It is worth noting that the institution in question is in a very remote location, not even accessed by proper roads and in winter an enormous effort is required sometimes just to reach it]. In 1993 and 1994 many died there from frost-bite. Often there were no windows, just plastic sheets. The drinking water was full of sand and the food was unpalatable. The well needed repairing. The Government was supposed to pay for the repair of the well but nothing happened. Everything froze there in the winter and the windows were always frozen on the inside. There was no water, no electricity and no food for quite a time. At that stage we took a number of people who lived there into our own home. So Larisa, Carolina and Vanya and others all came to us then. Some of them were converted and baptised in our church including those three. [Larisa, Carolina and Vanya all came to live in Casa Mea's houses in Sofia some years later and their lives changed completely in God's goodness. Vanya went to be with the Lord in February 2018. They never forget the kindness that had been shown to them in those early years by Brother Leonid and Sister Eugenia].

The staff in the institution hated the fact that we preached the Gospel to those there. They didn't want anything to do with us and they called us the anti-Christ. It was a costly work.

Some Christians from Holland began to help support the work they were doing there during the 1990s. Brother Leonid continues:

With their help we were able to provide some carpets for those in the institution. The Director was sometimes suspicious of us and we used to see lots of boxes of humanitarian aid in his office. But he did tell us that of all their visitors, we were the most persistent —that others had left but that we kept on visiting.

Our Dutch brethren sent beds and mattresses for the institution in the north. It was night time when these things arrived and we piled them on to our transport. We weren't thinking and during the long journey north fifteen mattresses dropped off! We had no chance of recovering them all, the distances were too great and they would already have been taken in any case. We feared God and knew that the humanitarian aid was given by Him. We would never have taken anything. My wife made fifteen mattresses to replace them!

We left for the States in 2006. It was very hard to leave those we knew there at the institution. We were very close to them. I can remember asking Larisa one day what she had eaten that day. She had eaten nothing but she said she had been nourished by the Word of God.

Sister Eugenia told me:

On 3rd September 1978, long before our work with children and adults had begun I was staying with my sister in Bălți. I had a vision for the first time. I was in front of our house in Sofia and in front of the house there were ten flames of fire with a serpent moving through the flames. In the foreground there were three fountains of water with pure, clean water flowing abundantly from them and flooding the area around them. It wasn't a dream, it was a vision. God was showing us what He was going to do.

ENOUGH FOOD FOR ALL

Brother Ilie also became involved in that same institution in those early years.

During the revival I understood very clearly that it was not enough to preach the Gospel—we had to live it and demonstrate its power in our lives. The first time I went to the institution in the north I cried. I was visiting with some Americans and those who lived there were starving. They were giving them sweets and they would eat the sweet papers too. I was disillusioned by the visitors' approach. At the same time I was asking the Lord why He had sent me there and a spiritual battle started within me which lasted about a month.

I was preaching in my church one Sunday in August 1993 and the Holy Spirit began to prompt me to share some of the things I had seen there. At the end of the service ten sisters surrounded me and said that they thought they could make a visit there themselves to take them food. We did exactly that and took them food soon afterwards. There were 530 people living there then including children and adults. We had not realised that there were also people in the isolation unit and when we got that far and forced the door open to gain access to them, to our dismay we realised that we had no food left for them.

The next Saturday we prepared enough food for all of them. And we had enough left over for another institution. After that we started to go every Saturday to feed them all. At that stage there were only 70 members in our church. However could we feed all those people? But God has His resources! I can remember we visited one Saturday in November and it was so cold and they had hardly any clothes and no shoes. I appealed to the people in our village and we collected a minibus full of shoes and clothing for them. We used to hold a service with them every Saturday. They so loved the services and the songs. We were always singing with them.

There had been no mattresses there since 1986. The Director said they needed 400 mattresses and at that time you could not have found so many mattresses in the whole of Moldova. I went to the Baptist Union for help to see if there were any international organisations which could help us. They gave me five addresses and I wrote off. One of the organisations, Dorcas from Holland, replied straight away and said they wanted to come on 7th January. I immediately agreed.

Two members of 'Dorcas' arrived in January 1994. It was very difficult with translation, but in February they sent us 400 mattresses and 400 beds together with cleaning materials and food. I learnt that I could fully trust in God. He is able to do more than we can think or imagine. After that we worked a lot with institutions all over the place.

The next chapter elaborates further on how work with adults and children with disabilities grew. It became the means of very many coming to the Lord.

19

ANOTHER WORK BEGINS

*B*rother Petru these days is one of the leaders of Christian camps for adults and children with disabilities and he is a powerful preacher. He also runs a day centre for children with disabilities which is where I met him. He gave the following account:

A small group of us used to meet for prayer regularly. One evening after such a prayer meeting I had a dream which I have never forgotten. I heard a voice saying to me, 'You need to take the Gospel to people with disabilities.' The voice said that they have a soul and also need to hear the Gospel and be saved. I said I had no contact with such people and however could I start such a work? It was 2001.

In 2003 despite many difficulties we set up a charity and registered it. We started a work and it grew and grew and soon we were helping 2000 people with disabilities. Christians from Switzerland helped us.

In 2004 we started the first camp in woods near Căpriana. We camped and it rained all week. About 90 people came to the first camp. We cooked over the open fire. We needed to find a good place for camp for people with disabilities which had good access to their rooms and to the dining hall and bathrooms. Eventually we found it at Călăraș. The owner did his utmost to help us and he created all the access we needed. The first camp at Călăraș took place in 2006 and 130 came. All of them were non-Christians but many were converted during that camp.

TELLING WHAT THE LORD HAD DONE

By 2007 there were two camps taking place, one for adults and another for parents and their children with disabilities. Each day as well as sports, games, crafts and gymnastics activities there are Bible studies, meetings for worship, singing and preaching and testimonies. There were always calls to repentance. Even at the very beginning about 40 were saved. They would go home and tell their husband or wife about what the Lord had done and then start to attend church with their spouse often. Many were later baptised and went on with the Lord. Helpers at the camps were being saved also. When people went home we put them in touch with evangelical churches near their homes. A Bible study correspondence course was started by Brother Sergiu. Very many camps have been held and very many have been brought to repentance and faith. Often the mothers who come are from Orthodox backgrounds. We don't attack their religion but just preach to them from the Bible.

A tall man came to camp with his daughter, Maria, who has Down's syndrome. His name is Sasha. He did not want to take part in the Bible study and stood at a distance away. His wife had died from cancer and he asked how we could talk about God and God's love when such things had happened to him. But after a while he became interested and he would listen at a distance. He went home and when he returned for the next camp he shared that he had been converted and baptised. We have known many times when the Lord has worked powerfully in the lives of individuals.

Another person was a young mother of 18 who had a child with severe cerebral palsy. Both the father and mother were very religious and went to the Orthodox Church often. We invited them to a service for children with disabilities at Christmas. The husband became a Christian first and then the mother was converted. She told us that she had suffered much from depression and had even considered suicide. But God worked and she started coming to the summer camps. She understood that God had used her child to save her. They had experienced such rejection over the years—even the medical staff told them to let the child die. When she told other mothers about how the Lord had worked in her life it was very powerful. The child died a few years ago.

I have visited these camps on a number of occasions. They take place in most pleasant locations with leafy trees providing welcome shade from the hot summer sun. Log cabins are scattered around the grounds for the camp which provide the sleeping accommodation. There is a swimming pool usually and a big outdoor meeting place for the services. Those adults we support in the houses of Casa Mea so look forward to going to these camps! People with disabilities in Moldova can live very restricted lives and many of those we know have little access to the outside world. These camps provide the most wonderful opportunities for them to meet with friends and to enjoy the activities and the services. During the warm summer evenings hundreds will sit listening to the preaching, participating in the singing and testimony times and praying. These services typically go on late into the night and nobody is keen for them to end. There is no doubt that they have been mightily used of God to encourage His people and to draw very many to know the Saviour. I know a number of people who have been converted at these camps. Brother Petru continues to play a key role in the leadership of the camps and will often preach during camp services. He went on to add a more personal note to his story:

OUR SON CHANGED MANY LIVES

In 2002 a child with Down's syndrome was born to us. They told us to leave him in the hospital and forget him as we had three other healthy children. I told them he was our child and we were taking him home. My wife had been told by God that the child she was expecting would change many lives. She imagined that he would be a great preacher. At that time families were hiding children who had disabilities. He did change a lot of lives and he was the main reason my wife started working with children with disabilities in the villages.

THE LORD'S CALL

Sister Lena about whom we heard earlier in Chapter 10 (she was converted at her husband's baptism), gave birth to a son who has autism. Her son Vasya is now 24 years old. This is Sister Lena's account:

I was invited to attend a meeting of other mothers of children with disabilities in 2005. That was when I felt a strong desire in my heart to serve them; it was the Lord calling me to work with them. I went home and I said to my husband Slava, 'I've found what I was looking for.' I knew that I could speak to these mothers about Jesus. It was the Lord who brought me to them. Not one of them was a believer then.

I started to look for practical help for these parents and approached all sorts of organisations. We encouraged them to go to Christian camps with their children as we knew that they would hear the Word of God there. A big group of us went together to a camp in 2006. After the camp in 2007 I proposed to the mothers that we should start a meeting for prayer and Bible study each week. There were about five of us in the beginning and we met in our home for the first year but then as we grew we moved to the church.

With time God extended our borders. We began to hold evangelistic services for families with children with disabilities. In the beginning about a hundred would come but these days about three hundred come to each of these services. Last Christmas two hundred children with disabilities came to our service. A number have been converted through our group and they have all been baptised. Two of them are people with disabilities, Roma and Olga. We started visiting an institution for adults with disabilities in the north of the country and I encouraged the mothers to come with me. With their own meagre resources they gathered enough money to feed the 500 people there! I was so moved by this. It was truly wonderful.

We have been to camps for people with disabilities in Belorussia three times together with mothers and their children and we have also been to three camps in the Ukraine. Five visits have been made to Smolensk in Russia and we have told them what the Lord is doing here amongst people with disabilities. There are 1 million people in the Smolensk region but only about 850 believers and the churches are small.

At the beginning of the work here we studied simple, essential subjects in our weekly meetings for prayer and Bible study such as the Ten Commandments. We wanted the teaching to be at the right level for the group that had gathered. We want to give all the glory to God for what He has done! He leads us and meets all our needs and gives us the means to help others. God takes care of us through others. It is enough.

A VERY GREAT JOY

I am very thankful to God that He brought this work into my life. My whole heart and soul is in the work and it is part of me. I often get tired and don't sleep at night thinking about how to conduct the work but when you see people seeking God and finding Him and wanting to make Him the Master of their lives all the tiredness disappears! And then you see parents able to thank God for the fact that they have a child with a disability. All this is a very great joy to me.

I long that more of them would hear the Word of God and that they would kneel before the Lord and find help there at His feet. They have many problems and I understand that well because I have experienced those difficulties too and still do. But I know that I have all the help I need in God and I feel His nearness and support in this work.

Not long ago we had organised a big evangelistic service and a lot of people were coming. I was leading the service and Brother Alexandru was going to preach. Just before the service was due to start my son Vasya began having convulsions.

He was given an injection and usually after this he will sleep for at least four hours. I was praying and crying out to the Lord, asking Him what I should do. I was overwhelmed with the situation. One hour after the injection Vasya opened his eyes and said, 'Church!' All praise to God! He gives us the strength to go on. All glory to Him!

For a number of years I have attended the prayer and Bible study group mentioned by Sister Lena. It meets on a Friday at midday for a couple of hours and attendance is always good. I never want to miss it if I can possibly avoid it! The small room in which we meet at the church is generally full. Prayer plays a very important part in the meeting and I do not think I will ever forget the fervent and persevering prayers of those mothers. Occasionally some fathers of children with disabilities will also attend. The Bible study time provides a wonderful opportunity for new Christians or for those seeking the Lord to ask questions they have and there are some lively discussions! Each evening at 8 p.m. individually in their own homes the women will join together in prayer again for all those attending the group and for their children. They have demonstrated a great capacity over the years to organise a range of outreaches often using their own resources sacrificially. Birthdays and national holidays are always celebrated with copious supplies of cake! A charity has been set up for the work which is called, 'My Child, My Blessing'. Our own charity, Casa Mea, works in close co-operation with them.

There had been a very sizeable Jewish population in Moldova prior to the Second World War and in 1990, before the exodus to Israel, America, Canada and Germany began, there were still a large number of Jewish people in the country. They were affected by the revival also as we shall discover in the next chapter.

20

JEWISH HISTORY IN MOLDOVA

*M*oldova has had a significant Jewish population in the past. In 1903 in the capital Chișinău, Jews made up about 45% of the city's population, numbering 50,000 out of a total population of 110,000. Jewish life flourished with Jewish schools in the capital educating 2000 pupils. There were pogroms [anti-Jewish riots] in 1903 and 1905. By 1930 the census records that there were 270,000 Jews in Moldova. After Germany conquered Basarabia in 1941, thousands of Jews were killed in mass shootings, deportations, ghettoes and concentration camps. [Basarabia was partly in the Ukraine, partly in Moldova. During most of the 1800s it was part of Russia and between World War 1 and 1940 it was part of Romania]. The Jewish population of Chișinău was nearly annihilated with 53,000 out of 65,000 Jews there perishing during the Second World War.

About 50,000 Jews have left the country from the late 1980's onwards, mostly to Israel, leaving only a few thousand in Moldova. As of 2014 there were about 15,000 Jews in Moldova with 10,000 of that number in Chișinău. I used to pass a large, derelict Hebrew school in Chișinău most days near the area that would have been the ghetto. Over the years I have known a number of men and women in Moldova whose ethnicity was Jewish but whose Jewish identity was generally suppressed. I usually discovered their Jewish roots by accident. I have visited one of the synagogues in Chişinău which is very centrally situated. A memorial to the Jewish victims of the Holocaust is to be found near the centre of the city. Those Jewish people who still remained in Moldova were also affected to some degree by the revival in the 1990s.

A NUMBER OF THEM REPENTED

I spoke to two men who were pastors of Messianic churches in Chişinău. This is the account of Brother Grigore who was one of them:

> Brother Mihai ordained me to the Messianic Church. Our congregation can be between sixty and a hundred but over the years so many have left for Germany, Israel and America. There is some Jewish blood in our family through my mother's line. I first became involved in Jewish ministry in 1993, when a Christian brother from America was visiting and was searching for a family grave. He found the grave in the Jewish cemetery. It was a huge cemetery and we found his grandfather's grave there. I can remember he prayed and cried when he found it. In those days there would have been about 20,000 Jews in Moldova.
>
> After that I organised a meeting for Jewish people in the Organ concert hall. Even the President of Moldova attended. The hall was full for the meeting! [This hall holds several hundred people]. They were happy to be there and a number of them repented at that very first meeting. I then thought about starting a work with the Jews.
>
> They were fearful and suspicious of meeting. I prayed. There is a society of those who were in the ghetto here in Chişinău and

who survived the concentration camps. I thought I would try to get a list of their names from the President of the Society. There were so many on that list then. Many have now left. I started to phone them all. I told them the date of a meeting and we met in a big room in School Number 2. I rented the room. It was the Passover. I phoned about 400 of them and told them we would celebrate the Passover. Almost all of them came! I said there would be music and we brought the choir and the orchestra from the church. It was wonderful! On that first occasion I spoke about the Passover from the Old Testament and they so rejoiced. I said that we would meet again.

Next month about 300 came to the meeting. We wanted to give them spiritual food and I spoke from the New Testament. Then we met the third and the fourth time. About 100 people were coming regularly. By that time the synagogue was warning people about me. They told them if they had contact with me they would not get the Rabbi's signature to get into Israel and they would not be permitted a Jewish burial.

Many Jews repented in the 1990s and even up to the present day that is happening although not to the same extent. Even this very day some of them have been asking me, 'How do we repent?' During the 1990s twelve or fourteen were being baptised at every baptism. I have a book with all their names in and where they have gone. Many have now died in old age. I do a great deal of home visiting. Often it takes about fifteen home visits before they will begin to open up. They are afraid to speak in bigger meetings. Exclusion from the synagogue is a very big threat and some of them have gone back as a result of this.

The first Rabbi was very harsh towards us but the present Rabbi is his son and is a bit kinder. I went to the Jewish school and they started to stone my car. There used to be towns with big Jewish populations such as Dubăsari, Călărași and Bălți. Dubăsari was started by a Jewish businessman named Dubasarschi. There was a terrible pogrom here in 1905 when jealousy of the Jews led to them being herded onto a ship one night after which they were all drowned. There were eighty synagogues here before 1905 and only seventeen afterwards—the rest were burned.

Another Messianic pastor I spoke to was Vladimir Moiseyev, the brother of the martyr Vanya.

NOT AN EASY WORK

I have been a pastor in a Messianic Church for the last 25 years. My father was Jewish. I long to bring Jewish people to Christ. It is not an easy work. Before you get to know a Jew you have to learn to listen to him. Sometimes he may decide that he does not want anything more to do with you. It always helps to offer him practical help like cleaning his floor if he is ill, or doing his washing up. On one occasion 73 Jewish people came to a service. I was astonished that so many wanted to come. I give them physical and spiritual food. The first Messianic Church in Chișinău was started in 1884. Iosif Rabinovici was the first pastor here in Chișinău. Today there are four Messianic churches here. Jewish identity passes down from generation to generation. So many were killed and it has often been forbidden for them to meet together. But today many of them have a living faith in Jesus Christ.

It is most wonderful to see the Lord bringing His ancient people to the Lord Jesus Christ. The awakening brought both Jews and Gentiles to the true Messiah.

I mentioned in the background notes to the book that reliable statistics with regard to church growth in the awakening are hard to obtain. Visible evidence of church growth however is apparent throughout Moldova, not least by the number of new church buildings. Chișinău itself has new church buildings in every sector of the city.

Pastor Nikolai whose church was planted in 1999, when they received a plot of ground on which to build, related the story of the building. They met outside through all weathers until the building was constructed. The cold weather did nothing to distract new people from coming to hear the message.

NEW CHURCH BUILDINGS

We were praying that we would be able to start building. A group came from the States and they had bought a large amount of bricks for a church in Găgăuzia only to discover that the church in question no longer needed them. A sister from our church overheard them speaking and she told them that our church could use them. It was enough bricks for us to build the church! We were overcome with joy and built with such joy! Then we saw miracle after miracle.

I never went abroad to gather funds, what we needed always arrived inexplicably. For example every evening after the building work, which we did with our own hands, we used to gather to pray. One evening we had no materials and no money left and there was no possible way out of the situation; it was the end of the road. We knelt down together on the ground and told the Lord we had nothing left and we asked Him to help us. Next morning at 11 a.m. a family approached us. They were Moldovan believers but they had never been to our church. They were members in Bethel. They told us that before they went to sleep the night before there was a sum of money which they decided they were going to take to the Bethel Church. They had a small business and always tithed. During the night the wife heard a voice telling her to take the money to the church in Ciocana. She questioned why she should take it to a church she had never visited when they were members at Bethel. Again the voice spoke and told her to take the money to Ciocana. This continued until 2 a.m. So in the morning the couple came to us and asked us what we were doing. They gave us $500. It was an immediate reply to our prayers! That family is in the States now.

There were so many instances like that. It was not just that God helped us materially step by step but at the same time the Lord was building the church spiritually. Our first baptism was 5th May 2000 when twelve were baptised. Since then there has not been a year when we did not baptise and our membership is now about 200 although very many have emigrated. The Lord made the church grow! His mercy has not come to an end. It is all the mercy of God; how He has cared for us! We understood that the Lord wanted to work.

Another pastor who leads a very large church in a vast, modern building shared with me:

The Lord called us to plant a church from nothing in Chişinău. My heart was given over to evangelism and I prayed. I wanted the first baptism to be the birth of the church. I chose the most populated area in Chişinău which did not have a Romanian church. This area is called Botanica. God confirmed this area in many ways. In my prayers I had asked the Lord for an apartment and for schools for the children very near. I found an apartment with four rooms at a modest rent of $50 a month and a school just behind the apartment which offered exactly the subjects the children needed. I started to teach English and I started to evangelise there.

Not far from the apartment was the Technical University and I started to teach there too. After nine months the first seven people were baptised. That was on 9th June 1996. I used our apartment for Bible studies and seven were converted through those meetings. They included two teachers, two students and three young mothers. It was very easy to get people to meet together then to study God's Word. People just flocked to hear the Word. We used to hold two, three or four baptisms of new believers every year. We grew to over 300 members and we used to meet in five different venues including a high school and a university.

It was a miracle how this building came into being and it was not without the most enormous struggle. There were so many obstacles but the Lord fought for us! I was threatened with a Kalashnikov not to buy this plot of ground. I also received a death threat from the Mafia. The Muslims offered me an enormous sum of money as they wanted to build a centre here. I refused because I knew for certain that the Lord wanted this place for the church building. My wife upheld me through all this and my children too. And the sisters in the church prayed—how they prayed for it all!

From this church we have planted another four churches, two Romanian and two Russian. We always concentrate on planting churches in villages and we always start with Bible study and prayer.

CHURCH GROWTH

As far as I can ascertain, in 1988 there were 126 Baptist churches in the country with 11,000 members. By 1994 there were 162 churches with 15,000 members. By 2000 there were 388 churches with 20,000 members. These figures do not reflect the enormous number of Christians who were emigrating from the country during this time. Neither do the figures include the growth in other Protestant denominations such as the Pentecostals nor the growth in the unregistered churches.

Our own work has been with adults with disabilities who have lived in institutions usually for decades and occasionally for their whole lives before coming to us. The last years have been years teeming with the miracles of God. Despite struggles and battles

MAUREEN WISE

without number we have seen the Lord providing four houses for
these friends of ours and working powerfully to bring them to
Himself. Some of their stories follow. I am more and more
convinced that the fruitfulness of the work to which God has
called us is a microcosm of the fruits of the revival.

21

MARIA'S STORY

*M*aria was in her 30s when she came to us and she arrived like a tornado! Of slight build, always on the move and having a moderate learning disability she moved into one of our houses in a village in the north of Moldova. Constantly active, she seemed to move at the speed of light and the solid front door was hanging off its hinges after a fortnight. Having lived in institutions almost all her life and without any family contact during that time, she had lived through experiences which horrified us. Deeply disturbed she would self-harm with anything she could find—a rusty nail from the garden, a piece of old glass—and her arms were covered in cuts. Left to her own devices she would have spent hours violently rocking to and fro in a dark room. I have rarely seen anybody rock to and fro with the speed and vehemence that Maria displayed. Clearly we did not want her to spend long periods of time in this kind of pursuit although we understood a little of the trauma that had caused her behaviour. Her language was of the gutter and her voice resounded at decibels throughout the house. We hardly knew what had hit us. Her expression resembled the classic unhappy emoticon most of the time. She hardly ever smiled.

Each of our four houses has a small-holding attached with land for fruit and vegetables and poultry and livestock are raised. [This would be typical in a Moldovan village]. Maria loved working on the small-holding and she quickly developed a very real interest in looking after the pigs, cows and poultry. These activities consumed some of her tremendous energies. At night she would collapse into an exhausted sleep. I think she must have been one of the very few people in Moldova to sleep through a recent earthquake! She sometimes stole from our neighbours which caused problems for us.

Sunday however was a day which Maria looked forward to. Church attendance was never obligatory but she did not hesitate to come along to the services in the small church. Dressed in her best attire, she managed to stay reasonably still during the long services and enjoyed learning the songs which she sang with gusto. At that time there was a young pastor in the church who preached the Word faithfully each Sunday. It was hard to know how much Maria understood, but she gave every appearance of listening and of being pleased to be there.

Staff found Maria's behaviour a constant challenge but they persevered with her. She took part in the prayer times in the houses and listened to the Word being read although she was unable to read. Maria loved singing Christian songs, not very tunefully but loudly. Time went on and we grew to love Maria despite being sometimes exasperated by her actions. We prayed much for her and felt for the suffering she had known throughout most of her life.

About two years after she first came to us Maria was in church as usual one Sunday morning. I was there also. At the end of the preaching from our beloved young pastor I watched as Maria went out to the front of the church and fell on her knees praying in a loud voice. I cannot recall all that she prayed but it was to the effect of, 'Lord Jesus take all the badness out of my heart! Make me clean and forgive me!' It was clear that Maria was in earnest in her praying. She was crying and unaware of the congregation around her. After the service the pastor spoke with her and we also did later that day. In the months that followed we watched her behaviour to see if there was evidence of a real change of heart. There was indeed!

Maria is still seriously loud and moves at bullet-like speed through this life. Her emoticon scowl is now much more often replaced by a broad smile. As with all of us, there are blips in her behaviour but the general trend is upwards. She loves to pray and she will talk about the Lord to anyone who is listening. Maria has recently been baptised. One of her frequently expressed phrases is, 'It was hell there [referring to the institution] but now it is like heaven.' When asked not long ago about her life now she said, 'I was sorry for my sins and I wanted to be with Jesus. The sisters love me here. No-one ever, ever beats you here. If you are told off for something we go forwards after that. I have been able to go out—to the Metro [the supermarket], to Chişinău, to camp at Călăraşi. The Word of God is here. I like football, swimming and running races.'

We rejoice that Maria has come to us and has left behind a life of great suffering. We see the love of a Saviour who has known her from all eternity and has drawn her in loving kindness to the Lord Jesus Christ and is preparing her for heaven. We believe that He will keep her by His power.

PRESENT WITH THE LORD

Vanya was born with no legs and he has cerebral palsy in his upper body. We had been told that as a baby he had been thrown out into a field where someone had found him and he had been placed in institutional care. Later on we did trace some of his family and discovered that one of his sisters was a school teacher.

The family did not choose to have contact with him. He needs help with every aspect of daily living. Vanya lived in institutions during the very worst years of economic collapse in the country and experienced hunger and cold and dreadful neglect very often. His friend, Gheorghe, would wheel him round the institution's grounds. Vanya would very frequently be tipped out of the wheelchair by others and would end up lying helplessly on the ground. Gheorghe would scoop him up in his arms and place him back in the wheelchair. During those desperate years Brother Leonid and Sister Eugenia about whom we read in Chapter 17, began to visit Vanya's institution. Vanya was converted through their ministry and was baptised in Brother Leonid's village church during the revival. When we held services in the institution, Vanya would always persuade someone to get him there and we could count on his presence. He continued to live in the institution but eventually moved to one of our homes along with Gheorghe and three other men.

Vanya had been terrified to move to us having been frightened by all sorts of stories from staff at the institution which painted us as fiends. He agreed to move on condition that if he did not like it, he could return immediately. We promised him that this would be the case. At the end of his first day with us Vanya was certain he wanted to stay!

Intellectually able, although physically dependent, Vanya's role would be to help the other men in the house understand what tasks needed to be done and oversee the successful completion of the various jobs. During the summer he loved to sit outside and observe comings and goings and chat to any visitors. He loved those times when a great crowd of visitors would descend on the house. Very politically aware he would keep us all informed of the latest political developments and the latest injustices and scandals. With bright blue eyes, the most beautiful smile and unending patience he played a key role in the house of which he became part. We were conscious that he was often in pain and winters presented a serious challenge, as we wondered if his weakened respiratory system would be strong enough for him to survive.

Vanya lived with us for nearly nine years and we trust that those years gave him a time which was in total contrast to the dreadful life he had experienced previously. Already a Christian when he came to us he was glad to attend the local church where he became a familiar face and a treasured member. Vanya died suddenly one Friday of a heart attack in February 2018 at the age of 47. The Sunday previously he had been in church and the pastor preached on the verse which says, 'Those whom He justified He also glorified' from Romans 8:30. The pastor who was preaching knew the men and women who lived in our houses in that village very well. He made a point of using their names and saying that whereas they have disabilities now, once they get to heaven there will be no problems with walking, or seeing, or any other kind of physical impediment. The men and women were all affected by what they had heard that morning. Vanya died the following Friday. We are absolutely certain that he is with the Lord who loved him and washed him with His own blood. Vanya is free for ever from pain and distress and full of joy in the glorious presence of the Saviour of sinners.

TWO CONVERSIONS

Ina was 32 years old and had been coming to our services in the institution for a long time. Often she would be first at the gate to welcome us. She had very short hair or her head was shaved because of lice, her clothes hung off her in a rag-bag kind of way and she would cling to anyone of us tightly as soon as we made an appearance. She was desperate for any kind of attention. This 'clinginess' got on the nerves of many people who lived in the institution and she became a regular target for beatings and abuse. There were frequently cuts and bruises on her face.

Ina loved to sing. She had a mild learning disability, although she made a great deal of sense when she spoke with us. Following the preaching on one particular morning Ina came to know the Lord. She said to us again and again, 'He loves me, He loves me!' 'He has forgiven me!' One of her favourite hymns and one she requested over and over again contains the refrain:

Do not leave me, do not leave me, Beloved Lord Jesus. Never ever leave me!

Her relationship with the Lord was real and impressed us each time we met her. When we went to her dormitory on a particular Saturday during one of our usual visits the atmosphere in the room was unusually quiet and sombre. Enquiring after the missing Ina, we were told to our horror, that she had died in hospital the previous day. The story was confused and we are unlikely ever to know the full account but it seems that she was kicked to death either by residents or staff or both and taken to hospital, but too late to save her life. Those in her dormitory referred to her that day as 'the one who believed in God.' What a testimony!

How our hearts grieved for Ina and for what she had suffered. We talked again and again about what she must have gone through in the period leading up to her death. Her mother (who had not visited for seven years and it turned out had a respectable career in the legal profession), came to collect Ina's body for burial in her home village.

Yet when we continued to dwell on Ina's tragic death we began to see something else. We began to realise that she was out of reach for ever of rejection , cruelty and beatings but that was not all. She had entered in through the gates into the City whose Builder and Maker is God. She had seen the King in His beauty. This King had set His love on her from eternity and had chosen her for Himself when so many others despised her. And our hearts became peaceful again.

More and more these days I become weary of my sin, weary of

the sin, suffering and sadness I see all around me and long for that holiness that will be revealed soon. We shall be like Him and in that place where sin shall be banished forever. What mighty power in our redemption that causes even us, with sins like scarlet, to be made as white as snow! We are going to be presented blameless and without fault and unreprovable in His sight!

Someone else who was converted about the same time as Ina was Sergiu. He is in his 30s and has cerebral palsy. His movements are uncoordinated and he uses a wheelchair which is in a state of gross disrepair. Painfully thin, I have often wondered how much food he receives in the most depressing room in which he lives with a number of other men. Those in that room, in common with those in many other rooms there, spend their daytimes staring listlessly into space or sleeping at the long table down one side of the room. There is hardly any communication and I suspect that Sergiu goes for very long periods without any human interaction at all.

He was in my sights one morning as a young man was preaching at a camp we were holding at the institution. The message being spoken was about our sins, secret and open, all being recorded by God and known to Him—as if they were all written on a long piece of paper. Then the preacher took the piece of paper he was holding as an illustration and tore it from top to bottom. He explained that every sin had been nailed to the Cross of Christ and that in His death He had taken every one of our sins in His body on the tree. We do not have to bear them anymore. Sergiu's face lit up as he understood the reality of this truth and discussions with him after the meeting indicated that the Lord had revealed Himself to him. The months that followed confirmed our view that he had been saved.

One day when we were visiting, Sergiu asked us if we had room for him in one of our houses. We had to explain that very sadly we did not at the time. He smiled and told us not to worry and pointed upwards and said, 'that's where my house is waiting for me.' We were awed by such simple acceptance and faith. Here was a powerful work of grace indeed.

In the next chapter we relate how some were baptised but only after they had believed on the Lord Jesus.

22

BAPTISMS, PRAYER AND FAITH

*S*even of the men and women in two of our houses were
due to be baptised. They had all been with us for some
years and we knew them very well. As far as we could tell there
had been a genuine work of God's grace in each of their lives. For
quite some time they had been longing to be baptised and then to
be admitted to take the Lord's Supper, but there had been delay
after delay. Now the time was approaching and the Sunday before
their baptism they were due to be questioned in front of their
local church.

The Sunday in question dawned. They all took the occasion
very seriously and had prepared as best they could with the help
of our staff. Arriving at church in a state of some apprehension,
they were asked to go out to the front of the church. They
huddled together for some moral support all dressed in their very
best clothes. Two of them were in wheelchairs.

The older pastor who questioned them knew them individually very well. He told the congregation how seriously he took his
responsibilities that day before God. You will understand that
those we support in the houses do not have extensive verbal skills
or a rich vocabulary. The pastor used simple but direct questions

for them in turn. Two of those questions and their answers follow:

Who is Jesus Christ?

- He made everything.
- He is the Son of God.
- He is alive.

What has He done for you?

- He made me clean.
- He washed me.
- He forgives me.
- He died on the Cross for me.
- He is living in my heart.

At the end of the questioning the church needed to vote for or against the proposed baptism of the candidates presented. A deacon spoke and turned to the congregation and said to us all, 'It is clear that the Holy Spirit has worked in all their lives. Who are we to prevent their baptism?' The church voted unanimously for them all to be baptised.

For me it was an indescribable privilege to hear their responses and to know that they believed those things with all their hearts and knew the Lord for themselves. By the end of their answers we were all in tears overwhelmed by the goodness and mercy of God. Ours is a God who chooses the weak things of this world to confound the things that are mighty.

STIRRING UP STRIFE

Mariana was one of those who was baptised the following Sunday. She had arrived on the same day as Maria at Casa Alex. We knew her superficially from the institution and she seemed to us to be a fairly amenable character from what we knew of her. In her late 30s, Mariana had some mild problems with mobility but in other respects was reasonably able. Unusually amongst those we supported she was able to read and write. Short of stature she had long, dark hair and a pleasant smile. Sometimes she had difficulty responding to questions and would look vacantly at us and lapse into silence.

It was not long before we discovered that Mariana harboured an intense dislike for two of the other people also living in the house. Such was her hatred for them that she could not bear to be in the same room as them! If she found herself in a situation where she had to communicate with them she would spit insults at them and use the foulest of epithets to address them. Not a situation liable to produce kind exchanges at the breakfast table as might well be imagined! (And we who prided ourselves on finding compatible friendship groups for the houses...)

Yet from the beginning Mariana expressed a desire to go to church regularly. The small village church had a young pastor who was on fire for God and preached simply and powerfully. She loved being in the church meetings and she even began to pray audibly at church meetings occasionally. I remember hearing her pray, 'Lord teach me how to repent!' But still her day to day behaviour did not change. Staff found her a handful, overtly complying with their requests but behind the scenes frequently stirring up trouble and amused when things went wrong as a result of her interventions.

As ever our only resort was prayer. We were fearful that we would lose valued staff as a consequence of her behaviour and our desperation caused us to cry out to the Lord for help yet again.

I REPENTED

I visited the house where Mariana lived very early in the New Year in 2013. A beaming Mariana met me at the door and took me into her room. There she opened a new Bible and showed me what she had written on the blank first page: '15th December 2013 I repented.' Mariana told me that she had knelt to ask the Lord to forgive her in church on that date and that she was His now. She said that she had also had a dream that she had been in a very dark wood crying. The Lord had approached her and asked her why she was crying and she told Him of all the things she had suffered in her life. He listened and told her that she was forgiven. How my heart rejoiced and praised the God who hears desperate prayers!

A PRAYER MEETING

Villages in Moldova often have a custom which means that one person will look after the entire village herd of cows on a particular day. Those owning cows will take it in turns to assume this responsibility. Over the years we have always had cows amongst our livestock attached to our houses in the north. On a certain morning, Gheorghe who lives in one of our houses, had taken the cow up to the pasture on the edge of the village and left her with the man responsible for that day. Alcoholism is a big problem in Moldova, in common with many countries in Eastern Europe. The person responsible for looking after the cows that day began drinking early and got more and more drunk as the day wore on. The cows, left to their own devices, began to help themselves to sugar beet which was piled high in the field. I had not known until that time that sugar beet is like arsenic to cows.

At the end of the day a sorry herd made its way back down the hill towards the village. Villagers arriving to collect their respective cows were horrified to discover the state of their animals, most of whom by then were very sick. A number of cows died after that episode and our own cow arrived home with a horn wrenched off and bleeding from her head and very sick indeed. As soon as she was in the barn she collapsed onto the floor and was unable to lift herself up again. Gheorghe and Mariana were most distressed to see her state as was everybody in the two houses the Lord has given us in that village.

A cow is a very valuable commodity in Moldova and I can remember that Anea and Liliana, my co-workers, and I discussed whether we should have the cow slaughtered immediately, for it not to be a complete financial loss to us. It was all a very real crisis.

The next morning early the cow was still very sick and it was impossible to find a vet willing to come to see her. Sister Viorica was working in Casa Matei, the men's house and had to go out for a short while. She returned to discover all the eleven occupants of the two houses standing in a wide circle in and around the barn where the cow was lying. She halted in her tracks as she came in through the gate into the courtyard, not understanding what was going on. Quickly she realised that she had stumbled into a prayer meeting! Mariana was standing in the barn with a Bible in her hand reading from a Psalm, then each person took it in turns to pray for the cow. Three of the people present were in wheelchairs and all of them had disabilities of one kind or another. No member of staff had orchestrated this prayer meeting. Sister Viorica told me that she was in tears as she listened to their prayers; they were oblivious to her presence until the prayer meeting ended.

That afternoon the cow got up on its feet and was taken for a walk round our grounds by Gheorghe. It completely recovered and gave birth to a succession of calves in the years that followed. The prayerfulness and faith of those we support in the houses has been a constant challenge to us. They trust with all their hearts in the invisible God who has infinite power and who hears their prayers.

DO YOU BELIEVE?

The opening of our fourth house, Casa Ana, provided another platform for the exercise and increase of faith. It was scheduled for a Saturday in October 2016 and we were expecting a great crowd to the opening service and the ribbon-cutting celebration. I think about ten people were due to fly out from the UK that Friday to participate, as well as very many friends who were due from different places in Moldova. Six women had been chosen to be the residents of the new house. About two weeks before the opening service we were told by the authorities that there was not the slightest possibility that the six women would be able to move by the opening date because of various bureaucratic impediments that looked completely non-negotiable. The stuff of which nightmares are made began to form in my head. A new, beautiful purpose built house, staff appointed, preaching, music and food organised, visitors invited, air tickets purchased and none of the six women at the opening service! The UK visitors included someone who had been sent by the mission I worked with, UFM, to film the proceedings! My anxiety levels began to shoot through the ceiling...

At the time I was reading through Matthew's Gospel in my daily readings. I had reached Matthew 9 and I read 'Believe ye that I am able to do this?' The words came into my consciousness with great power. It was as if the Lord was asking the question directly of me, 'Do you believe that I am able to do this?' Did I believe that the Lord could so work that the women would somehow be allowed to move into the new house by the time of the opening? Could I believe that seemingly unsurpassable obstacles could be removed to allow this to happen? I reflected on the One who was asking me and I knew that with all my heart I believed He could do this. I replied to Him in the same way as the blind men had replied in Matthew 9:28, 'Yea Lord'. Yes Lord, I believe with all my heart that you can do this. My spirit was quietened and from that point on I had a complete conviction and peace that the Lord would act. The panic left.

The Thursday evening before the opening service on the Saturday, we received a phone call from the Government officials. (Remember that the UK visitors were flying in on the Friday, the following day). We were told that we could move five of the women into the house on the Friday and that the sixth would follow very shortly!

Do you believe that I am able to do this? Yes Lord.

23

THE LORD CAME IN POWER

J hope that you have been able to glimpse a little of this extraordinary work of God in a small country which is unknown to most people. Following a long period of persecution for Christians and during a time of political turmoil, and enormous economic hardship the Lord visited Moldova in power. When the awakening began the context was one in which pastors had received no theological training and did not have access to theological books. Even Bibles had been in short supply.

In the West we have at our disposal the most amazing treasure of rich theological literature. We are fed by the Word of God regularly in our churches, by pastors called of God. Opportunities for theological training abound. Our theology would often be what is known as 'Reformed' and perhaps there is sometimes a hint of unspoken satisfaction and pride in our theological prowess. There is a great Christian hymnology going back centuries.

Moldova had none of these benefits when the revival began. It would be easy to criticise some of their church practices and theological emphases if one had a mind to. We are very adept at highlighting theological shortcomings on minor issues. But it was in such a setting, with a paucity of theological training and literature, that the Holy Spirit came down in great power, creating a heart thirst for the Saviour and for the Word. It was there that men and women and children were drawn to the Lord Jesus Christ in their hundreds and thousands. They experienced a visitation marked by celestial fire.

These things have challenged me as I have written. So many men and women I know in Moldova, including those I have interviewed, unknowingly communicate to me a sense of passion and zeal for Christ and costly dedication to His service. Their lives and their conversation are full of Christ and they bring the fragrance of Christ with them. They have become living sacrifices who yearn to bring others to their Saviour. There is an unconscious selflessness about their conduct which communicates Christian love most powerfully. I sometimes wonder what it would take to bring our congregations to our knees in the UK? What would it take to bring us believers to deep repentance?

I have tried to give some small insight into the incredible fruit of the awakening. As we have seen, this encompasses a great missionary vision eastwards, a flourishing of theological training and countless efforts to reach those in great need with the Gospel. God has manifestly blessed those outreaches.

In terms of our own work with adults with disabilities, we are acutely conscious that what has happened over the years, in terms of the conversion of many of them, the provision of houses and the growth of a work is nothing to do with us. We often feel as though we have to pinch ourselves to comprehend the remarkable things we have witnessed. What is clear to us is that we have been allowed to see a breaking in of Divine power. Nothing else explains what has happened and it was one of the fruits of the revival. We do not have words sufficiently to praise Him.

Revive Thy work O Lord
Thy mighty arm make bare
Speak with the voice that wakes the dead

And make Thy people hear!

Revive Thy work O Lord
Disturb the sleep of death;
Quicken the smouldering embers now
By Thine almighty breath!

Revive Thy work O Lord
Create soul thirst for Thee
And hungering for the Bread of Life
O may our spirits be!

Revive Thy work O Lord
And give refreshing showers;
The glory shall be all Thine own
The blessing Lord be ours!

— ALBERT MIDLANE